I SEE YOU

DR. MAYANK BHATNAGAR

INDIA · SINGAPORE · MALAYSIA

ISBN 979-8-89277-943-2

DEDICATED TO

ALMIGHTY,MY BELOVED FAMILY Members & Well Wishers....

Special Thanks

Jatin Bhatnagar

CONTENTS

PREFACE

Malware, in its various forms, has become an increasingly pervasive threat in the digital age. With each passing day, hackers and cybercriminals devise new ways to exploit vulnerabilities, compromise systems, and steal sensitive data. As a result, the field of malware analysis has emerged as a critical discipline in the realm of cybersecurity.

This book, titled "I See You," is an endeavor to provide a comprehensive guide to understanding, analyzing, and combatting malware. Whether you are an aspiring cybersecurity professional, a seasoned IT expert, or simply someone intrigued by the inner workings of malicious software, this book is designed to equip you with the knowledge and skills needed to navigate the intricate landscape of malware.

Through the pages of this book, you will embark on a journey that delves into the core principles of malware analysis. Starting with the basics, you will explore the significance of malware analysis, its goals, and the ethical considerations that accompany this crucial practice. As you progress, you will uncover the diverse types of malware and the stages of their lifecycles, gaining insights into their behaviors and techniques.

Practicality is at the heart of this book. You will learn how to set up a controlled malware analysis environment, employing various tools and technologies to dissect both static and dynamic aspects of malicious code. From static analysis, which scrutinizes the structure of malware without execution, to dynamic analysis, which involves observing the behavior of malware in action, you will gain a holistic understanding of the techniques used to decipher the intent and impact of malicious programs.

In the spirit of a hands-on approach, the book will guide you through case studies that dissect real-world examples of malware. You will have the opportunity to analyze ransomware, examine banking Trojans, reverse engineer advanced persistent threats, and explore mobile malware, unraveling the complex strategies employed by cyber adversaries.

Emerging trends are a crucial aspect of any field, and malware analysis is no exception. This book ventures into the realms of fileless malware analysis, IoT malware intricacies, cloud-based analysis, and the infusion of artificial intelligence in understanding and countering malware.

To ensure that knowledge gained from this book is readily applicable, it delves into best practices and practical tips. From establishing a malware analysis workflow to effective documentation and staying up-to-date with the constantly evolving threat landscape, this section equips you with the tools to not only analyze malware but also contribute to a more secure digital world.

The journey concludes with a bibliography, providing a collection of resources that have shaped the creation of this book. Please note that while this outline serves as an initial blueprint, the final content will be entirely unique, developed with an unwavering commitment to originality and ethical standards.

As you delve into the pages ahead, may you find empowerment in understanding the mechanics of malware and the strategies to mitigate its impact. In a world where technology drives progress, knowledge becomes our most potent armor against those who would seek to exploit it.

Chapter 1

INTRODUCTION TO MALWARE ANALYSIS

1.1 WHAT IS MALWARE?

Malware, short for malicious software, refers to any software or code that is specifically designed to harm, exploit, or gain unauthorized access to computer systems, networks, or user devices. It is a broad term that encompasses various types of malicious programs, including viruses, worms, Trojans, ransomware, spyware, adware, and botnets.

Malware is created with malicious intent by cybercriminals and attackers who aim to compromise the integrity, confidentiality, and availability of digital systems. It can target individual users, businesses, government entities, or any organization connected to the internet.

The primary characteristics of malware include:

1. Malicious Intent: Malware is intentionally designed to perform harmful actions, such as stealing sensitive information, disrupting system operations, controlling infected devices, or spreading to other systems.

2. Self-Replication: Some types of malware, such as viruses and worms, have the ability to replicate and spread across systems autonomously, infecting other files, devices, or networks.

3. Covert Execution: Malware often operates silently and covertly to avoid detection. It may hide within legitimate files, masquerade as benign applications, or exploit vulnerabilities in software to execute its malicious code.

4. Payload and Behavior: Malware performs various malicious activities based on its intended purpose. This can include stealing passwords, logging keystrokes, encrypting files for ransom, launching distributed denial-of-service (DDoS) attacks, or creating backdoors for remote access.

5. Evolving Techniques: Malware authors continually adapt their techniques to evade detection and bypass security measures. They employ sophisticated obfuscation, encryption, and anti-analysis techniques to make it challenging for security analysts to analyze and detect their malware.

Malware can be distributed through various means, including malicious email attachments, infected websites, software downloads from untrusted sources, drive-by downloads, social engineering tactics, or exploiting software vulnerabilities.

Understanding the nature of malware is essential for effective cybersecurity. Malware analysis, as a discipline, focuses on studying the behavior, structure, and functionality of malware to develop countermeasures, detect infections, and protect systems from potential threats. By comprehending the intricacies of malware, security professionals can better defend against attacks, respond promptly to incidents, and mitigate the potential damage caused by malicious software.

1.2 IMPORTANCE OF MALWARE ANALYSIS

Malware analysis plays a crucial role in the field of cybersecurity and is essential for understanding, detecting, and mitigating the risks posed by malicious software. Here are several key reasons why malware analysis is of utmost importance:

1. Threat Intelligence and Understanding: Malware analysis provides valuable insights into the nature, behavior, and capabilities of different types of malware. By studying malware samples, security professionals gain a deeper understanding of attack vectors, propagation methods, and the motives of attackers. This knowledge helps in developing effective defense strategies and staying ahead of evolving threats.

2. Detection and Identification: Malware analysis enables the detection and identification of malicious software within

systems, networks, or individual devices. By analyzing the code, behavior, and artifacts associated with malware, security analysts can create signatures and detection rules for antivirus software, intrusion detection systems (IDS), and other security tools. This aids in promptly identifying and mitigating malware infections.

3. Incident Response and Forensics: When a security incident occurs, such as a malware infection or a data breach, malware analysis plays a vital role in incident response and forensic investigations. Analyzing the malware involved in an incident helps in understanding the scope of the attack, identifying affected systems, and uncovering the attacker's techniques and objectives. This information is critical for containing the incident, remediating affected systems, and strengthening defenses against future attacks.

4. Vulnerability and Patch Management: Malware analysis helps identify software vulnerabilities exploited by malware. By understanding the attack techniques and exploits used, organizations can prioritize their patch management efforts and apply security updates to mitigate vulnerabilities. This proactive approach minimizes the risk of malware exploiting known weaknesses in systems or software.

5. Malware Classification and Taxonomy: Malware analysis aids in categorizing and classifying different types of malware based on their behavior, propagation methods, and payloads. This classification helps in building comprehensive threat intelligence databases and allows security professionals to develop specific countermeasures and mitigation strategies for different malware families.

6. Development of Security Tools and Technologies: Malware analysis serves as the foundation for developing advanced security tools and technologies. By reverse engineering and analyzing malware samples, security researchers can identify new attack techniques, develop innovative detection mechanisms, and improve existing security solutions. This continuous cycle of analysis and tool development strengthens the overall security posture of organizations.

7. Awareness and Training: Malware analysis contributes to raising awareness among users, organizations, and the cybersecurity community about the risks and consequences of malware. Through the dissemination of analysis reports, case studies, and best practices, security professionals educate users about safe computing practices and help them recognize and respond to potential threats effectively.

In summary, malware analysis is essential for understanding the ever-evolving landscape of malware, detecting infections, responding to incidents, and developing effective defense strategies. By delving into the intricacies of malware, security professionals can enhance their ability to protect systems, networks, and data from malicious software and minimize the impact of cyberattacks.

1.3 GOALS OF MALWARE ANALYSIS

The goals of malware analysis revolve around gaining a deeper understanding of malicious software, identifying its behavior and capabilities, and developing effective countermeasures to mitigate the risks associated with malware. Here are the key goals of malware analysis:

1. Understand Malware: The primary goal of malware analysis is to gain insight into the inner workings of malware. This includes understanding its functionality, propagation methods, communication channels, and potential impact on compromised systems. By dissecting malware, security professionals can uncover the techniques and tools employed by attackers, providing valuable intelligence for defense strategies.

2. Detect and Identify Malware: Malware analysis aims to develop techniques and tools to detect and identify malware instances within systems, networks, or individual devices. This involves analyzing the code, behavior, and artifacts associated with malware to create signatures, rules, or machine learning models for effective detection. By accurately identifying malware, security teams can take appropriate action to mitigate the risks and prevent further compromise.

3. Reverse Engineer Malicious Code: Reverse engineering is a critical aspect of malware analysis, focusing on understanding

the underlying logic and algorithms used by malware authors. This involves deconstructing the malware's binary code, extracting meaningful information, and reconstructing the program's logic and functionality. Reverse engineering enables deeper analysis, identification of vulnerabilities, and the development of effective countermeasures.

4. Develop Countermeasures: Malware analysis aims to develop effective countermeasures and mitigation strategies against malware. This includes the development of signature-based detection methods, behavior-based detection mechanisms, and the creation of security tools and technologies that can detect, block, or neutralize malware threats. The goal is to improve the overall security posture and resilience of systems and networks.

5. Enhance Incident Response: Malware analysis is crucial in incident response, helping organizations effectively handle security incidents involving malware. By analyzing the malware involved in an incident, security teams can understand the scope of the attack, determine the compromised systems, and identify the attacker's techniques and objectives. This information guides incident containment, remediation, and the formulation of response strategies.

6. Contribute to Threat Intelligence: Malware analysis contributes to threat intelligence by sharing insights, research, and analysis with the wider cybersecurity community. By documenting and sharing analysis reports, security researchers help create a collective knowledge base that aids in understanding emerging threats, identifying attack trends, and developing proactive defense measures.

7. Support Legal and Law Enforcement Efforts: Malware analysis plays a vital role in supporting legal and law enforcement efforts against cybercriminals. Analysis results can provide crucial evidence in legal cases, aid in identifying threat actors, and contribute to the dismantling of malicious infrastructure. Malware analysts may collaborate with law enforcement agencies, sharing their expertise and insights to combat cybercrime effectively.

By achieving these goals, malware analysis strengthens the ability to detect, respond to, and mitigate the risks posed by malicious software. It empowers organizations to proactively defend against malware threats and contributes to the overall security and resilience of systems, networks, and digital environments.

1.4 LEGAL AND ETHICAL CONSIDERATIONS

When engaging in malware analysis, it is essential to adhere to legal and ethical guidelines. Malware analysis involves studying and manipulating potentially harmful software, and it is crucial to conduct these activities within the boundaries of applicable laws, regulations, and permissions. Here are the key legal and ethical considerations in malware analysis:

1. Compliance with Laws and Regulations: Malware analysts must comply with relevant laws and regulations related to computer security, data protection, intellectual property rights, and privacy. It is essential to understand and abide by the legal frameworks established by local, regional, and national authorities.

2. Obtaining Proper Authorization: Performing malware analysis should be done with appropriate authorization. This could involve seeking consent from system owners, network administrators, or relevant stakeholders before conducting analysis activities on their systems or networks. Unauthorized access or analysis is not only illegal but also unethical.

3. Respect for User Privacy: Malware analysts must respect user privacy and handle any sensitive or personally identifiable information (PII) in accordance with applicable privacy laws and regulations. It is crucial to handle data securely and protect the privacy of individuals who may be affected by the analysis process.

4. Secure Handling of Malware Samples: Malware samples used for analysis should be handled securely to prevent unintended dissemination or accidental infections. Analysts must ensure that proper safeguards are in place to contain and isolate malware samples, preventing them from spreading or causing harm to other systems or networks.

5. Confidentiality and Non-Disclosure: Malware analysts often work with sensitive and confidential information. It is essential to maintain the confidentiality of any proprietary or classified information obtained during the analysis process. Non-disclosure agreements (NDAs) may be required when collaborating with third parties or sharing analysis findings.

6. Responsible Information Sharing: Sharing analysis findings, research papers, or reports should be done responsibly and ethically. Malware analysts should consider the potential impact of sharing information, such as disclosing vulnerability details or aiding malicious actors. Responsible information sharing helps the broader cybersecurity community stay informed and develop effective countermeasures.

7. Continuous Professional Development: Malware analysts should stay up to date with the evolving legal and ethical landscape. This can be achieved through continuous professional development, attending relevant training, and participating in industry conferences and forums. Staying informed about legal requirements and ethical best practices is essential for responsible and effective malware analysis.

By adhering to these legal and ethical considerations, malware analysts contribute to a safe and secure digital environment. Responsible and lawful practices not only protect the rights and privacy of individuals but also promote trust and cooperation within the cybersecurity community.

Chapter 2

FUNDAMENTALS OF MALWARE ANALYSIS

The fundamentals of malware analysis encompass the basic principles and techniques used to analyze and understand malicious software. This process involves examining the behavior, structure, and functionality of malware to uncover its intentions, capabilities, and potential impact. Here are the key fundamentals of malware analysis:

1. Malware Collection and Preparation: Malware analysis begins with obtaining malware samples for analysis. Samples can be collected from various sources, such as infected systems, honeypots, malware repositories, or security research organizations. Once collected, the samples need to be properly prepared and isolated to prevent accidental infections or unintended spread.

2. Static Analysis: Static analysis involves examining the malware without executing it. This includes analyzing the code, file structure, and metadata of the malware sample. Techniques such as file header analysis, disassembly, and examining strings and resources within the binary provide insights into the malware's structure, potential functionality, and possible indicators of compromise (IOCs).

3. Dynamic Analysis: Dynamic analysis involves executing the malware in a controlled environment, such as a virtual machine or a sandbox, to observe its behavior. This includes monitoring system calls, network traffic, file system activity, registry modifications, and any other actions performed by the malware. Dynamic analysis helps uncover the malware's runtime

behavior, such as its propagation methods, communication channels, and payload execution.

4. Behavioral Analysis: Behavioral analysis focuses on understanding the actions and effects of the malware on the infected system. It involves observing and documenting the malware's behavior, such as creating or modifying files, accessing sensitive information, communicating with external servers, or manipulating system settings. Behavioral analysis helps in identifying the potential impact of the malware and the associated risks.

5. Code Analysis and Reverse Engineering: Code analysis and reverse engineering involve examining the malware's binary code to understand its internal logic, algorithms, and potential vulnerabilities. Techniques such as disassembly, debugging, and code deobfuscation are used to analyze the malware's functionality, identify encryption or obfuscation techniques, and discover any hidden features or backdoor capabilities.

6. Malware Family Classification: Malware analysis aims to classify malware into specific families or categories based on similarities in behavior, code patterns, or characteristics. This classification helps in understanding the relationships between different malware samples and aids in developing effective detection and mitigation strategies.

7. Indicator Extraction: Malware analysis involves extracting indicators of compromise (IOCs) from the analyzed malware. These can include file hashes, IP addresses, domain names, mutexes, registry keys, or specific patterns observed in the malware's behavior. IOCs help in creating detection signatures and rules for antivirus systems, intrusion detection systems (IDS), and other security tools.

8. Reporting and Documentation: Malware analysis should be thoroughly documented, including all findings, observations, and analysis techniques used. Analysis reports serve as a record of the analysis process and provide valuable information for incident response, forensic investigations, and sharing knowledge within the cybersecurity community.

9. Continuous Learning and Adaptation: Malware analysis is an ever-evolving field, and staying up to date with the latest malware trends, techniques, and countermeasures is crucial. Malware analysts need to engage in continuous learning, participate in training programs, attend conferences, and collaborate with other professionals to enhance their skills and knowledge.

By following these fundamentals, malware analysts can gain a comprehensive understanding of malicious software, detect and mitigate malware threats effectively, and contribute to the broader goal of securing digital systems and networks.

2.1 TYPES OF MALWARE

Malware, short for malicious software, encompasses a wide range of malicious programs designed to compromise systems, steal data, or disrupt normal computer operations. Here are some of the most common types of malware:

1. Viruses: Viruses are self-replicating programs that infect other files or systems by attaching themselves to host files. They spread when the infected files are executed, often by exploiting vulnerabilities or through user interaction. Viruses can cause damage to files, slow down system performance, and spread to other connected devices.

2. Worms: Worms are standalone programs that spread across networks or through removable media without the need for user interaction. They exploit security vulnerabilities to replicate themselves and infect other systems. Worms can consume network resources, propagate rapidly, and carry payloads that can harm systems or steal information.

3. Trojans: Trojans, named after the famous Trojan Horse, disguise themselves as legitimate or desirable software but contain malicious code. Once installed, Trojans can perform various malicious actions, such as stealing sensitive information, creating backdoors for remote access, or delivering other types of malware.

4. Ransomware: Ransomware is a type of malware that encrypts files or locks down systems, rendering them inaccessible to users

until a ransom is paid. It often spreads through malicious email attachments, infected downloads, or exploit kits. Ransomware attacks can lead to significant data loss, financial losses, and operational disruptions.

5. Spyware: Spyware is designed to secretly monitor a user's activities, gather sensitive information, and transmit it to a remote attacker. It can capture keystrokes, log browsing habits, record passwords, or take screenshots without the user's knowledge. Spyware is often used for identity theft, espionage, or unauthorized surveillance.

6. Adware: Adware, short for advertising-supported software, is a type of malware that displays unwanted advertisements on a user's system. It may come bundled with legitimate software and can redirect web browsers, modify search results, or generate intrusive pop-up ads. While not always harmful, adware can degrade system performance and compromise user privacy.

7. Botnets: Botnets are networks of compromised computers, also known as zombies or bots, controlled by a central command-and-control (C&C) server. They can be used to carry out coordinated attacks, send spam emails, launch distributed denial-of-service (DDoS) attacks, or perform other malicious activities without the owner's knowledge.

8. Rootkits: Rootkits are designed to gain unauthorized access and control over a computer system while remaining hidden from detection. They modify the operating system or firmware to provide backdoor access, disable security mechanisms, and maintain persistence. Rootkits are often used to facilitate other types of malware or for unauthorized system administration.

9. Keyloggers: Keyloggers capture and record keystrokes made on a compromised system, allowing attackers to collect sensitive information such as passwords, credit card details, or personal data. Keyloggers can be implemented as software or hardware, and they can be used for identity theft, financial fraud, or unauthorized access.

10. Fileless Malware: Fileless malware operates in memory without leaving traces on the hard disk. It leverages legitimate system

processes or scripting engines to carry out malicious activities, making it challenging to detect and remove. Fileless malware often exploits vulnerabilities in software or uses social engineering techniques to infiltrate systems.

These are just some examples of the diverse range of malware types encountered in the digital landscape. Understanding the characteristics and behaviors of different malware types is crucial for effective detection, prevention, and mitigation strategies in the field of cybersecurity.

2.2 MALWARE LIFECYCLE

The lifecycle of malware refers to the various stages that a malicious software program goes through, from its creation to its execution and eventual removal. Understanding the malware lifecycle helps in comprehending the progression of malware and implementing effective defense strategies. Here are the key stages of the malware lifecycle:

1. Creation and Development: The first stage involves the creation and development of the malware by cybercriminals or malicious actors. This stage may include writing the malicious code, designing the payload, and implementing evasion techniques to bypass security measures. The malware creators often employ programming languages, exploit kits, or malware construction kits to build their malicious software.

2. Distribution and Delivery: Once the malware is developed, the next stage is distributing and delivering it to target systems. Malware can be distributed through various methods, including email attachments, malicious websites, infected downloads, or social engineering techniques. The goal is to entice users into executing or accessing the malware, often by disguising it as legitimate files or enticing content.

3. Execution and Installation: Once the malware successfully infiltrates a target system, it proceeds to execute and install itself. This stage involves the activation of the malicious code and the placement of necessary files or registry entries to establish persistence. The malware may employ techniques such as code injection, file dropping, or exploiting vulnerabilities to gain control over the compromised system.

4. Command and Control (C&C): After installation, the malware establishes a connection to a command-and-control (C&C) server operated by the attacker. The C&C server acts as a communication hub, allowing the attacker to send commands, receive updates, and control the infected systems remotely. This stage enables the attacker to maintain control over the compromised network and issue instructions to the malware.

5. Malicious Activity: Once the malware is connected to the C&C server, it carries out its intended malicious activities. These activities can vary depending on the type and purpose of the malware. Examples include stealing sensitive data, launching DDoS attacks, encrypting files for ransom, propagating to other systems, or providing unauthorized access to the attacker.

6. Persistence and Evasion: Malware aims to maintain persistence on the compromised system to ensure continued control and avoid detection. It employs various techniques to evade detection by security software, such as rootkit installation, anti-analysis measures, or encrypting its own code. Persistence techniques include creating startup entries, modifying system settings, or hiding within legitimate processes.

7. Detection and Analysis: As malware carries out its malicious activities, it becomes susceptible to detection by security software or human analysts. Detection may occur through signature-based scanning, behavioral analysis, network monitoring, or security incident response. Detected malware samples are then analyzed to understand their behavior, capabilities, and potential impact on the compromised systems.

8. Mitigation and Removal: Once detected, malware needs to be mitigated and removed from the infected systems. This stage involves employing appropriate countermeasures, such as applying security patches, updating antivirus software, blocking network communications, or conducting malware removal procedures. Removal can be challenging, especially for persistent or advanced malware, requiring specialized tools and techniques.

9. Post-Infection Analysis and Remediation: After malware removal, post-infection analysis is conducted to determine the extent of the damage, identify vulnerabilities that led to the infection, and implement remediation measures. This includes patching vulnerabilities, updating security configurations, educating users, and enhancing network defenses to prevent future infections.

10. Evolution and Adaptation: The lifecycle of malware continues with the evolution and adaptation of malicious software. As security measures improve and detection techniques evolve, malware creators modify their tactics, techniques, and procedures (TTPs) to evade detection and maintain effectiveness. This ongoing cycle drives the need for continuous research, analysis, and innovation in the field of cybersecurity.

Understanding the stages of the malware lifecycle helps in developing proactive defenses, implementing effective detection and prevention mechanisms, and responding to malware incidents promptly. By staying ahead of the evolving threat landscape, organizations and individuals can mitigate the risks posed by malware and protect their digital assets.

2.3 MALWARE DETECTION TECHNIQUES

Detecting malware is a crucial aspect of cybersecurity, as it allows for the identification and mitigation of potential threats. Various techniques and technologies are employed to detect and analyze malware. Here are some common malware detection techniques:

1. Signature-based Detection: Signature-based detection relies on predefined signatures or patterns of known malware. Antivirus software uses these signatures to scan files, memory, or network traffic for matching patterns. If a signature match is found, the file or activity is flagged as malicious. This technique is effective against known malware but may struggle with new or modified variants.

2. Heuristic Analysis: Heuristic analysis involves the use of behavioral and rule-based algorithms to identify potentially malicious behavior. It detects malware based on characteristics or patterns commonly exhibited by malicious software, even if

no specific signature is available. Heuristic analysis can identify previously unknown malware, but it may also generate false positives or miss sophisticated threats.

3. Machine Learning: Machine learning algorithms are trained on large datasets to identify patterns and behaviors indicative of malware. They can detect both known and unknown malware by analyzing features such as file attributes, code behavior, network communication, or system anomalies. Machine learning models require continuous training and refinement to keep up with evolving malware techniques.

4. Sandbox Analysis: Sandbox analysis involves executing suspicious files or programs within a controlled environment known as a sandbox. The sandbox isolates the activity from the production system, allowing analysts to observe the behavior of the malware without risking infection. Sandbox analysis provides insights into the malware's actions, including network connections, file modifications, or attempts to evade detection.

5. Behavior-based Detection: Behavior-based detection focuses on monitoring the runtime behavior of software to identify malicious activities. It involves analyzing system events, network traffic, registry modifications, and other behavioral indicators. Deviations from normal behavior patterns or the presence of known malicious actions can trigger alerts or flag suspicious activities for further investigation.

6. Reputation-based Detection: Reputation-based detection relies on reputation databases that maintain information about the trustworthiness of files, websites, or IP addresses. It assigns reputation scores based on historical data, user feedback, or security community reports. If a file or entity has a poor reputation score, it is considered potentially malicious. Reputation-based detection can quickly identify known malicious entities but may have limited effectiveness against new threats.

7. Anomaly Detection: Anomaly detection techniques establish a baseline of normal behavior and identify deviations that may indicate the presence of malware. Statistical analysis, machine

learning, or rule-based algorithms are employed to detect unusual network traffic, system activity, or user behavior. Anomaly detection helps identify previously unknown or zero-day malware but requires continuous monitoring and tuning to reduce false positives.

8. YARA Rules: YARA (Yet Another Recursive Acronym) is a powerful pattern matching tool used to create and share rules for malware detection. YARA rules define specific patterns or characteristics of malware, such as strings, file headers, or code snippets. These rules are then used to scan files, memory, or network traffic for matches, enabling the detection of specific malware families or behaviors.

9. Memory Analysis: Memory analysis focuses on examining the contents of a system's memory to identify and extract malicious code or artifacts. It can uncover hidden processes, injected code, rootkit activity, or other forms of memory-based malware. Memory analysis techniques include process monitoring, examining process memory dumps, or using specialized tools to detect and analyze malware in memory.

10. Threat Intelligence: Threat intelligence involves gathering and analyzing information about current and emerging threats. It provides insights into known malware campaigns, attacker techniques, compromised infrastructure, or indicators of compromise (IOCs). Integrating threat intelligence feeds into security systems enables proactive detection and response to evolving malware threats.

Effective malware detection often involves a combination of these techniques, using multiple layers of defense to increase the

chances of detecting and mitigating malicious software. The continuous evolution of malware necessitates the adoption of robust detection mechanisms and the integration of threat intelligence to stay ahead of emerging threats.

2.4 MALWARE ANALYSIS METHODOLOGIES

Malware analysis is the process of dissecting and understanding malicious software to gain insights into its behavior, functionality, and potential impact. Various methodologies and techniques are employed to conduct effective malware analysis. Here are some commonly used malware analysis methodologies:

1. Static Analysis: Static analysis involves examining the malware without executing it. It focuses on analyzing the structure, code, and other characteristics of the malware file. Techniques used in static analysis include:

   * File Header Analysis: Analyzing the file headers to gather information about the file type, format, and potential indicators of maliciousness.

   * Disassembling and Decompiling: Transforming the binary code into assembly language or high-level programming language representations for better understanding and analysis.

   * Code Review: Examining the code logic and identifying suspicious or malicious functions, API calls, or code snippets.

   * String Analysis: Extracting and analyzing strings within the malware to uncover potential indicators of malicious behavior, such as URLs, IP addresses, or encryption keys.

   * Resource Analysis: Analyzing resources embedded within the malware, such as images, configuration files, or embedded executables.

   Static analysis helps in identifying potential malicious characteristics, understanding the code structure, and gathering initial insights about the malware's functionality.

2. Dynamic Analysis: Dynamic analysis involves executing the malware in a controlled environment to observe its behavior and interactions with the system. Techniques used in dynamic analysis include:

   * Sandbox Analysis: Running the malware in an isolated environment (sandbox) to monitor its behavior, network communication, file modifications, and system interactions. Sandbox analysis helps in understanding the malware's execution flow, payload delivery, or potential damage.

* Debugging: Attaching a debugger to the malware to monitor its runtime behavior, analyze memory changes, track API calls, and identify potential vulnerabilities or exploits used by the malware.

* Network Traffic Analysis: Capturing and analyzing network traffic generated by the malware to identify communication with command-and-control (C&C) servers, data exfiltration, or other malicious activities.

* System Monitoring: Observing system-level events, such as process creation, registry modifications, or file system changes, to identify suspicious behavior or indicators of compromise.

Dynamic analysis provides a deeper understanding of the malware's behavior, its interaction with the environment, and the potential impact on the compromised system.

3. Hybrid Analysis: Hybrid analysis combines elements of both static and dynamic analysis methodologies. It leverages the strengths of each approach to gain a comprehensive understanding of the malware. Hybrid analysis involves:

* Initial Static Analysis: Conducting preliminary static analysis to gather information about the malware's structure, file type, and potential indicators.

* Execution and Monitoring: Running the malware in a controlled environment to observe its behavior, system interactions, and network communications.

* In-depth Static Analysis: Conducting further static analysis on the malware's code, resources, or other characteristics to gain additional insights.

* Code Reversing: Reverse engineering critical parts of the code to understand its functionality, encryption methods, or anti-analysis techniques.

Hybrid analysis allows for a more thorough analysis, combining the benefits of static and dynamic techniques to reveal the malware's capabilities, persistence mechanisms, and potential countermeasures.

4. Automated Analysis: Automated analysis involves leveraging specialized tools, sandboxes, or threat intelligence platforms to automate the analysis process. Automated analysis techniques include:

    ❋   Malware Sandboxes: Using automated sandboxes to execute malware samples and collect behavioral data, network traffic, and system modifications for analysis.

    ❋   Behavioral Signatures: Developing behavioral signatures or indicators of compromise (IOCs) based on the observed behavior of malware samples.

    ❋   Machine Learning: Employing machine learning algorithms to analyze large volumes of malware samples, detect patterns, and classify malware families.

    ❋   Threat Intelligence

        Integration: Integrating automated analysis systems with threat intelligence feeds to correlate observed malware behavior with known threats.

        Automated analysis helps in scaling the analysis process, reducing manual effort, and enabling rapid detection and response to emerging malware threats.

5. Reverse Engineering: Reverse engineering involves deconstructing the malware to understand its inner workings, algorithms, and encryption methods. Reverse engineering techniques include:

    ❋   Disassembling and Decompiling: Transforming the malware's binary code into human-readable assembly language or high-level programming language code.

    ❋   Code Reversing: Analyzing the decompiled code to understand the malware's logic, algorithms, encryption, or anti-analysis techniques.

    ❋   Memory Analysis: Examining the malware's code and data structures in memory to identify hidden processes, injected code, or rootkit activity.

✳ Patch Analysis: Analyzing patches or modifications made by the malware to identify vulnerabilities it exploits or anti-analysis measures it employs.

Reverse engineering helps in understanding the malware's functionality, identifying potential vulnerabilities, and developing countermeasures.

It's important to note that malware analysis methodologies can vary depending on the goals, resources, and expertise of the analyst or organization. A combination of these methodologies and techniques provides a comprehensive approach to malware analysis, enabling the understanding of the malware's behavior, impact, and potential mitigation strategies.

Chapter 3

SETTING UP A MALWARE ANALYSIS ENVIRONMENT

Creating a proper malware analysis environment is crucial for conducting effective and secure analysis of malicious software. Here are the key steps to set up a malware analysis environment:

1. Isolation: Malware analysis should be performed in an isolated environment to prevent the spread of infections and protect sensitive systems. Consider the following isolation measures:

    a. Use a dedicated physical or virtual machine: Set up a separate machine solely dedicated to malware analysis. This helps contain any potential infections within a controlled environment.

    b. Air-gapped or segmented network: Connect the malware analysis machine to a separate network that is isolated from production networks. This prevents accidental spread of malware to other systems.

    c. Disable or restrict network access: Configure the malware analysis machine to limit its network connectivity. Block outgoing connections, except for necessary communication with security tools or internet access for research purposes.

    d. Use a virtualization platform: Utilize virtualization software such as VMware, VirtualBox, or Hyper-V to create isolated virtual machines for different analysis scenarios.

2. Baseline System: Establish a baseline system configuration that represents a clean, fully patched, and updated environment.

This allows for comparisons and identification of changes caused by malware.

a. Install a clean operating system: Install the desired operating system version on the malware analysis machine, ensuring it is a clean and legitimate installation from a trusted source.

b. Patch and update the system: Apply all available operating system patches, service packs, and security updates to ensure the system is up to date.

c. Install essential tools: Install essential analysis tools such as debuggers, disassemblers, network monitoring tools, virtualization software, and sandboxing tools.

3. Malware Analysis Tools: Equip the malware analysis environment with necessary tools to facilitate analysis and investigation. Some commonly used tools include:

a. Debuggers: Tools like OllyDbg, IDA Pro, or WinDbg help in analyzing the behavior of malware, examining code execution, and identifying potential vulnerabilities.

b. Disassemblers and Decompilers: Tools like Ghidra, IDA Pro, or Hopper assist in reverse engineering malware by converting binary code into readable assembly language or high-level programming languages.

c. Sandbox and Virtualization Tools: Tools like Cuckoo Sandbox, VMware, or VirtualBox enable the execution of malware samples in isolated environments for behavioral analysis.

d. Network Monitoring Tools: Tools like Wireshark or tcpdump capture and analyze network traffic generated by malware, helping identify communication channels and potential command-and-control activity.

e. File Analysis Tools: Tools like PEStudio, VirusTotal, or YARA assist in examining file attributes, identifying potential indicators of compromise, and scanning files for known malware signatures.

4. Security Controls: Implement security controls to protect the malware analysis environment and prevent any accidental compromise:

    a. Antivirus and Endpoint Protection: Install a reliable antivirus software with up-to-date signature databases on the malware analysis machine to provide an additional layer of protection.

    b. Network Segmentation: Use firewalls or network segmentation techniques to isolate the malware analysis environment from production networks, preventing lateral movement of malware.

    c. Access Controls: Implement strong access controls for the malware analysis environment, including strong passwords, two-factor authentication, and limited user privileges.

    d. Data Storage and Backup: Establish secure data storage and backup procedures to ensure preservation of malware samples and analysis artifacts while maintaining confidentiality and integrity.

5. Documentation and Reporting: Maintain detailed documentation of the analysis process and findings to support future investigations and knowledge sharing. This includes:

    a. Malware Sample Information: Document details about the analyzed malware, such as file names, hashes, source of acquisition, and any associated information.

    b. Analysis Steps and Results: Document the steps performed during the analysis, including static and dynamic analysis findings, observed behavior, network activity, and identified indicators of compromise.

    c. Reporting: Prepare comprehensive analysis reports that summarize the findings, potential impact, and recommendations for mitigating the threat.

By following these steps and establishing a well-equipped and isolated malware analysis environment, analysts can effectively examine and understand the behavior of malicious software while minimizing the risk of compromising production systems.

3.1 ISOLATED TESTING ENVIRONMENT

Creating an isolated testing environment is essential for safely analyzing and testing malware samples without risking the compromise of production systems. An isolated testing environment provides a controlled space where malware can be executed and observed without affecting critical assets. Here are some key considerations when setting up an isolated testing environment:

1. Physical or Virtual Isolation:

    * Physical Isolation: Use dedicated physical machines specifically designated for malware analysis. These machines should not be connected to the production network and should have limited physical access.

    * Virtual Isolation: Utilize virtualization technologies such as VMware, VirtualBox, or Hyper-V to create isolated virtual machines (VMs) for malware analysis. Each VM can have its own network configuration, operating system, and analysis tools.

2. Network Segmentation:

    * Separate Network: Create a dedicated network segment for the isolated testing environment. This can be achieved by setting up a separate VLAN or using network segmentation techniques.

    * Firewall Rules: Implement strict firewall rules to restrict inbound and outbound connections between the testing environment and the production network. Only allow necessary communication channels for analysis purposes.

3. Offline Analysis:

    * Air-Gapped Environment: For highly sensitive or advanced malware, consider setting up an air-gapped environment that has no physical or network connections to the internet or any external networks.

    * Network Traffic Monitoring: If internet access is required for analysis, use network monitoring tools like Wireshark

or a network proxy to capture and analyze the network traffic generated by malware samples.

4. Virtual Machine Snapshots:

   * Snapshot Feature: Take advantage of the snapshot functionality provided by virtualization platforms. Before executing a malware sample, create a snapshot of the clean VM state. This allows you to revert back to the original state after analysis, eliminating any potential system modifications caused by malware.

5. Limited Privileges and User Accounts:

   * User Privileges: Limit user privileges within the testing environment. Use non-administrator or standard user accounts to execute malware samples, reducing the impact of potential malicious activities.

   * User Access Control: Implement strong user access controls, including strong passwords and two-factor authentication, to prevent unauthorized access to the testing environment.

6. System Monitoring and Logging:

   * Monitoring Tools: Deploy system monitoring tools to capture and log system activities during malware analysis. This includes monitoring process creation, file system modifications, registry changes, and network connections.

   * Centralized Logging: Store the logs generated during analysis in a centralized and secure location for future reference and analysis.

7. Malware Sample Management:

   * Secure Storage: Establish a secure storage system for storing malware samples. Use password-protected or encrypted archives to prevent accidental leakage or unauthorized access.

   * Proper Naming and Tagging: Implement a systematic naming convention and tagging system for malware samples. Include relevant information such as file names, source, date, and any associated metadata.

8. Regular Updates and Patching:

   ✳ Operating System Updates: Keep the testing environment's operating system and software up to date with the latest security patches and updates to minimize vulnerabilities.

   ✳ Analysis Tools Updates: Stay updated with the latest versions of analysis tools and antivirus software to ensure the best possible protection and detection capabilities.

By following these practices, an isolated testing environment can provide a secure and controlled environment for analyzing and testing malware samples. It helps prevent accidental infections, minimizes the impact of malware, and protects critical systems and data from potential threats.

3.2 TOOLS AND TECHNOLOGIES

When setting up a malware analysis environment, it is important to have the right set of tools and technologies that aid in the analysis process. These tools and technologies enable analysts to examine and understand the behavior of malware samples effectively. Here are some commonly used tools and technologies in malware analysis:

1. Debuggers and Disassemblers:

   ✳ IDA Pro: A widely used interactive disassembler and debugger that allows for in-depth analysis of malware code, data structures, and control flow.

   ✳ OllyDbg: A powerful debugger that enables dynamic analysis of executable files, helping analysts understand the behavior of malware during runtime.

   ✳ x64dbg: An open-source debugger for Windows executables that provides a user-friendly interface and supports both x86 and x64 architectures.

2. Sandboxing and Virtualization Tools:

   ✳ Cuckoo Sandbox: An open-source automated malware analysis system that utilizes virtualization to execute and monitor malware samples in an isolated environment. It provides detailed reports on malware behavior and network communication.

- ✲ VMware Workstation: A popular virtualization platform that allows the creation of virtual machines for running malware samples in a controlled environment. It offers snapshot capabilities for easy system restoration.
- ✲ VirtualBox: An open-source virtualization tool that provides similar capabilities to VMware, allowing the creation of isolated virtual machines for malware analysis.

3. Network Analysis Tools:
   - ✲ Wireshark: A widely used network protocol analyzer that captures and analyzes network traffic generated by malware. It helps in identifying communication channels, command-and-control activity, and data exfiltration.
   - ✲ tcpdump: A command-line packet sniffer that captures network traffic and saves it to a file for later analysis. It provides detailed information about network packets, aiding in the investigation of malware behavior.
4. Static Analysis Tools:
   - ✲ PEStudio: A tool for analyzing Windows executable files. It examines file headers, imports, exports, resources, and other characteristics to identify potential indicators of compromise.
   - ✲ Dependency Walker: A utility that displays the dependencies of a Windows executable, helping analysts understand the libraries and functions used by malware.
   - ✲ YARA: A powerful pattern matching tool used for creating and sharing malware detection rules. It enables the identification of known malware based on specific patterns or characteristics.
5. Dynamic Analysis Tools:
   - ✲ Procmon: A process monitoring tool from Sysinternals that captures and logs system events, including process creations, file system activity, and registry modifications. It helps in understanding malware behavior and system interactions.

* Process Explorer: Another tool from Sysinternals that provides detailed information about running processes, their loaded modules, open files, and network connections. It assists in identifying suspicious or malicious processes.

6. Threat Intelligence Platforms:

* VirusTotal: A web-based platform that aggregates multiple antivirus scanners and other analysis tools to scan and analyze files for potential malware. It provides information on detected threats and behavioral patterns.

* ThreatConnect: A threat intelligence platform that collects, analyzes, and shares threat intelligence data. It helps analysts identify known threats, understand their characteristics, and correlate them with malware samples.

7. Automation and Scripting:

* Python: A popular programming language used in malware analysis for automating repetitive tasks, developing custom analysis scripts, and integrating with various analysis tools and libraries.

* PowerShell: A scripting language for Windows systems that can be used to automate analysis tasks, interact with the operating system, and analyze suspicious PowerShell scripts often employed by malware.

These tools and technologies, combined with proper knowledge and expertise, enhance the capabilities of malware analysts and expedite the analysis process. It is important to stay updated with the latest versions of these tools and leverage their features to effectively analyze and understand malware behavior.

3.3 VIRTUAL MACHINES AND SANDBOXING

Virtual machines (VMs) and sandboxing are integral components of a malware analysis environment. They provide a controlled and isolated environment for executing and analyzing malware samples without risking the compromise of the host system. Here's a closer look at virtual machines and sandboxing in the context of malware analysis:

1. Virtual Machines:

   * Virtualization Technology: Virtual machines emulate an entire computer system, including the operating system, hardware, and software components, within a host machine. This allows for the creation of multiple isolated environments on a single physical system.

     Benefits of Virtual Machines:

   * Isolation: VMs provide a high level of isolation, ensuring that any malware executed within a VM does not impact the host system or other VMs.

   * Snapshot Capability: Virtualization platforms offer snapshot functionality, enabling analysts to capture the state of a clean VM before executing a malware sample. This allows for easy restoration to the original state after analysis.

   * Resource Management: VMs allow for easy allocation and management of system resources such as CPU, memory, and disk space, ensuring optimal performance during analysis.

   * Environment Reproducibility: VMs ensure that the same analysis environment can be replicated across different systems, promoting consistency and facilitating collaboration.

     Popular Virtualization Platforms:

   * VMware Workstation: A commercial virtualization platform that provides a robust set of features for creating and managing VMs.

   * VirtualBox: An open-source virtualization tool that offers similar capabilities to VMware and is widely used for malware analysis.

   * Hyper-V: A virtualization technology developed by Microsoft, commonly used on Windows-based systems.

2. Sandboxing:

   * Sandbox Technology: Sandboxing involves running malware samples within a controlled environment that restricts their access to the underlying system resources. Sandboxes

typically employ a combination of virtualization, system monitoring, and behavioral analysis techniques.

Benefits of Sandboxing:

* Behavior Monitoring: Sandboxes monitor the behavior of malware during execution, capturing system interactions, file modifications, registry changes, and network activity.

* Dynamic Analysis: Sandboxing provides a dynamic analysis environment, allowing analysts to observe the real-time behavior of malware samples without exposing the host system to potential harm.

* Risk Mitigation: By executing malware within a sandbox, the impact of malicious activities is contained and does not affect critical systems or sensitive data.

Popular Sandboxing Tools:

* Cuckoo Sandbox: An open-source automated malware analysis system that utilizes virtualization and behavioral analysis techniques to examine the behavior of malware samples.

* FireEye Sandbox: A commercial sandboxing solution that offers advanced analysis capabilities, including code execution, network monitoring, and memory analysis.

* Joe Sandbox: A comprehensive malware analysis platform that combines dynamic analysis, code deobfuscation, network traffic analysis, and static analysis techniques.

Both virtual machines and sandboxing provide valuable benefits for malware analysis. Virtual machines offer a broader scope of analysis, allowing for the examination of malware in a complete system environment. On the other hand, sandboxing provides a more focused and controlled environment specifically designed for analyzing malware behavior and identifying potential threats.

The choice between virtual machines and sandboxes depends on the specific analysis requirements, available resources, and the analyst's expertise. In practice, a combination of both approaches is often employed to leverage the strengths of each method and maximize the effectiveness of malware analysis.

Chapter 4

STATIC MALWARE ANALYSIS

Static malware analysis is a crucial phase in the process of analyzing malicious software. It involves examining the structure, characteristics, and content of malware without executing it. Static analysis provides valuable insights into the nature of the malware, its functionality, and potential indicators of compromise. Here are some key techniques and tools used in static malware analysis:

1. File Identification and Metadata Analysis:

    *   File Type Analysis: Identify the file type of the suspicious file, such as PE (Portable Executable) for Windows executables, APK for Android applications, or DMG for macOS disk images.

    *   Metadata Extraction: Extract metadata from the file, including file name, size, creation date, and modification date. This information can provide initial clues about the nature and origin of the file.

2. Hash-based Analysis:

    *   Hash Calculation: Calculate the cryptographic hash of the file using algorithms like MD5, SHA-1, or SHA-256. Compare the hash with known malicious or legitimate file hashes to determine if it is a known threat or benign file.

    *   Hash Lookups: Use online services or databases like VirusTotal, which maintain large collections of file hashes associated with known malware. These services can provide insights into the reputation and prevalence of the analyzed file.

3. Code Analysis:

   ✳ Disassembly: Disassemble the binary file to obtain the assembly instructions. Tools like IDA Pro, radare2, or objdump can assist in this process.

   ✳ Reverse Engineering: Analyze the disassembled code to understand the functionality, control flow, and logic of the malware. Identify key functions, API calls, and potential malicious behavior.

4. String Analysis:

   ✳ String Extraction: Extract strings from the binary file, including hardcoded URLs, IP addresses, file names, registry keys, or other identifiable information. These strings can reveal important details about the malware's behavior and potential targets.

   ✳ Encoding and Obfuscation: Identify any obfuscated or encoded strings within the malware. Decrypt or decode them to reveal their true content and purpose.

5. Resource Examination:

   ✳ Resource Extraction: Extract embedded resources, such as images, configuration files, or additional executable files, from the malware. Analyze these resources for any hidden information or malicious payloads.

   ✳ Manifest Analysis: For Windows executables, examine the manifest file to identify requested permissions, required libraries, or potential vulnerabilities.

6. Anti-Analysis Techniques:

   ✳ Packaged and Compressed Files: Detect if the malware is packed or compressed using tools like UPX or PEiD. Unpack or decompress the file to reveal its original content for analysis.

   ✳ Code Obfuscation: Look for obfuscated code or anti-analysis tricks designed to hinder static analysis. These techniques may include code encryption, junk code insertion, or control flow obfuscation.

7. Signature-based Detection:

    ✻ Signature Creation: Create custom signatures based on unique patterns, byte sequences, or characteristics of the malware. Use tools like YARA to develop and apply these signatures for efficient detection of similar malware samples in the future.

8. Automated Analysis Tools:

    ✻ Malware Analysis Sandboxes: Submit the suspicious file to automated malware analysis platforms like Cuckoo Sandbox, Joe Sandbox, or Hybrid Analysis. These sandboxes execute the file in a controlled environment and provide reports on its behavior, network activity, and potential indicators of compromise.

Static malware analysis provides valuable insights into the inner workings of malicious software. It helps identify the type of malware, its potential capabilities, and aids in developing detection and mitigation strategies. It is important to combine static analysis with other techniques, such as dynamic analysis and behavioral analysis, to gain a comprehensive understanding of the malware's behavior and potential impact.

4.1 FILE ANALYSIS

File analysis is a fundamental component of static malware analysis. It involves examining the structure, content, and characteristics of a suspicious file to gain insights into its nature and potential malicious behavior. File analysis helps in understanding the file's purpose, identifying potential indicators of compromise, and determining the appropriate analysis techniques. Here are the key steps involved in file analysis:

1. File Type Identification:

    ✻ Determine the file type: Identify the file format based on its file extension or magic number. Common file types include executables (PE files for Windows, Mach-O for macOS), scripts (such as PowerShell or JavaScript), documents (e.g., PDF, Word), archives (ZIP, RAR), and more.

* Analyze the file header: Examine the file header to gather information about the file format, version, and other metadata. This information aids in determining the appropriate analysis techniques and tools.

2. Metadata Examination:

   * Extract file metadata: Retrieve metadata associated with the file, such as file name, size, creation date, modification date, and author information. This metadata can provide initial insights into the file's origin and potential purpose.

   * Analyze digital signatures: Check for the presence of digital signatures within the file, especially for executables and digitally signed documents. Verify the authenticity and integrity of the signatures to determine if the file has been tampered with or comes from a trusted source.

3. Static Code Analysis:

   * Disassemble the file: Disassemble the file's code, especially for executable files, to obtain the assembly instructions. Tools like IDA Pro, radare2, or objdump can assist in disassembling the code.

   * Reverse engineer the code: Analyze the disassembled code to understand its functionality, control flow, and potential malicious behavior. Identify important functions, system API calls, and potentially suspicious or obfuscated code.

4. String Analysis:

   * Extract strings: Extract strings from the file, including URLs, IP addresses, file paths, registry keys, or any other textual information embedded within the file. These strings can reveal potential indicators of compromise or provide insights into the file's behavior and purpose.

   * Analyze encoded or obfuscated strings: Identify any encoded or obfuscated strings within the file. Decrypt or decode them to reveal their true content and uncover any hidden information or malicious payloads.

5. Resource Examination:

   ✷ Extract embedded resources: Investigate the presence of embedded resources within the file, such as images, configuration files, or additional executables. Analyze these resources for any hidden data or potential malicious content.

   ✷ Analyze manifest files: For Windows executables, examine the manifest file to identify requested permissions, required libraries, or potential vulnerabilities. The manifest can provide valuable information about the file's intended behavior and dependencies.

6. Anti-Analysis Techniques:

   ✷ Detect file packing or compression: Determine if the file is packed or compressed using tools like UPX or PEiD. Unpacking or decompressing the file can reveal its original content for further analysis.

   ✷ Identify code obfuscation: Look for obfuscated code or anti-analysis tricks designed to hinder static analysis. These techniques may include code encryption, junk code insertion, or control flow obfuscation. Deobfuscate the code to understand its true functionality.

7. Signature-based Detection:

   ✷ Create custom signatures: Develop custom signatures based on unique patterns or characteristics observed in the file. Use tools like YARA to create and apply these signatures for efficient detection of similar malware samples in the future.

File analysis is a critical step in understanding the nature and potential risks associated with a suspicious file. It provides insights into the file's purpose, behavior, and potential impact on the system. By carefully examining the file's structure, metadata, code, strings, and resources, analysts can uncover valuable information to inform further analysis and aid in the development of detection and mitigation strategies.

4.2 METADATA EXAMINATION

Metadata examination is an important aspect of static malware analysis that involves extracting and analyzing metadata associated with a file. Metadata provides valuable information about the file's origin, properties, and potential risks. By examining metadata, analysts can gain insights into the file's authenticity, integrity, and potential indicators of compromise. Here are the key steps involved in metadata examination during malware analysis:

1. File Properties:

    * File Name: Analyze the file name to determine if it appears suspicious or follows a naming convention commonly associated with malware. Malicious files often use deceptive or enticing names to trick users into executing them.

    * File Size: Note the file size as it can be an initial indicator of suspicious behavior. Unusually large or small file sizes may suggest the presence of packed or obfuscated code.

    * File Extension: Examine the file extension to understand the file format and associated applications. Malware authors often attempt to disguise malicious files by using benign-sounding extensions.

    * Creation and Modification Dates: Note the timestamps indicating when the file was created and last modified. Unusual timestamps, such as recent modifications on system files or executables, may raise suspicion.

2. File Hashes:

    * Calculate Hashes: Calculate cryptographic hash values, such as MD5, SHA-1, or SHA-256, to uniquely identify the file. Hash values act as digital fingerprints and can be compared against known malicious or legitimate file hashes.

    * Hash Lookups: Compare the file's hash against hash databases, such as VirusTotal, to determine if it matches any known malware samples. These databases aggregate information from various antivirus vendors and can provide insights into the file's reputation and potential risks.

3. Digital Signatures:

    *   Certificate Analysis: If the file is digitally signed, examine the digital certificate associated with the file. Verify the certificate's authenticity, issuer, and expiration date. A valid digital signature from a trusted entity indicates the file's integrity and reduces the likelihood of tampering or malicious modifications.

    *   Certificate Revocation: Check if the certificate has been revoked by the issuing authority. Revoked certificates indicate a loss of trust and may suggest potential risks associated with the file.

4. File Metadata:

    *   Author and Company Information: Extract metadata that indicates the author or company associated with the file. This information can help determine if the file originates from a reputable source or if it has been tampered with.

    *   Version Information: Identify version numbers and other software-related metadata that can aid in determining the file's purpose, compatibility, and potential vulnerabilities.

    *   Internal File Paths: Analyze any internal file paths or directory structures referenced within the file. These paths may reveal important information about the file's dependencies or potential malicious activities.

5. Document Metadata (For Document Files):

    *   Office Documents: For document files (e.g., PDF, Word, Excel), examine document metadata such as author names, creation dates, and revision history. Malicious actors may attempt to hide malicious content or macros within these documents.

    *   Hidden Data: Analyze hidden or deleted content within documents that may contain sensitive or malicious information. Tools like OfficeMalScanner or Document Inspector can assist in extracting and analyzing hidden data.

Metadata examination provides valuable context and initial insights into a file's properties, origin, and potential risks. By analyzing file names, sizes, extensions, hashes, digital signatures, and other metadata, analysts can make informed decisions about the next steps in the malware analysis process. It is important to combine metadata examination with other analysis techniques, such as code analysis and dynamic analysis, to gain a comprehensive understanding of the file's behavior and potential impact.

4.3 REVERSE ENGINEERING

Reverse engineering is a vital technique used in static malware analysis to gain a deeper understanding of the inner workings of malicious software. It involves dissecting the code and behavior of a malware sample to uncover its functionality, algorithms, and potential vulnerabilities. Reverse engineering allows analysts to uncover hidden or obfuscated code, identify malicious behavior, and develop effective detection and mitigation strategies. Here are the key steps involved in reverse engineering malware:

1. Disassembling the Code:

    * Disassemble the executable: Use a disassembler tool, such as IDA Pro, radare2, or objdump, to convert the machine code of the executable file into assembly language instructions.

    * Analyze the assembly instructions: Study the disassembled code to understand the program's flow, logic, and structure. Identify important functions, system API calls, and potential areas of interest.

2. Identifying Entry Points:

    * Locate the main entry point: Identify the initial code execution point within the malware. This entry point is often the starting point for malicious activities and can provide insights into the malware's behavior and purpose.

    * Identify key functions and routines: Identify functions or routines that handle critical operations, such as file manipulation, network communication, encryption/ decryption, or process injection. These functions are often crucial for the malware's malicious behavior and warrant closer analysis.

3. Control Flow Analysis:

   * Understand program flow: Analyze the flow of the program by tracing the execution paths of instructions and identifying decision points, loops, and branching conditions. This analysis helps in understanding the control flow logic and potential variations in the malware's behavior.

   * Resolve indirect calls and jumps: Reverse engineer and resolve any indirect calls or jumps in the code to determine the targets and destinations. This helps in identifying potential function calls to system APIs or other important routines.

4. Decompilation and High-Level Analysis:

   * Decompilation: Convert the disassembled assembly code back into a higher-level language representation, such as C or C++. Decompilers like Ghidra, RetDec, or Hex-Rays IDA can assist in this process.

   * Analyze decompiled code: Study the decompiled code to gain a more abstract and readable view of the malware's functionality. This analysis can reveal the purpose of specific code blocks, data structures, and algorithmic operations.

5. Data Flow Analysis:

   * Identify data sources and sinks: Analyze how data flows through the malware to identify potential sources (user input, network data) and sinks (file writes, network communication). This helps in understanding how the malware collects information, communicates, or performs malicious actions.

   * Track data dependencies: Trace the flow of critical data variables within the code to identify how they are processed, modified, or used. This analysis can reveal important data transformations, encryption/decryption routines, or data storage mechanisms.

6. Uncovering Anti-Analysis Techniques:

   * Identify code obfuscation: Look for obfuscated or encrypted code designed to evade analysis. Reverse engineer and deobfuscate the code to understand its true functionality.

* Handle anti-debugging and anti-VM techniques: Identify any anti-debugging or anti-virtual machine techniques employed by the malware to hinder analysis. Reverse engineer and bypass these techniques to continue the analysis process.

7. Patching and Behavior Modification:

* Patching for analysis: Modify the malware's code to disable or modify certain behavior, allowing for safer analysis within a controlled environment. This technique helps in observing the malware's activities without risking the host system's security.

* Behavior modification: Reverse engineer the malware to understand its potential capabilities, such as keylogging, data exfiltration, or remote command execution. This analysis helps in developing appropriate countermeasures and detection strategies.

8. Reverse engineering:

Reverse engineering is a complex and time-consuming process that requires a deep understanding of programming languages, operating systems, and malware techniques. It allows analysts to unravel the inner workings of malware, identify its capabilities and intent, and develop effective countermeasures. However, it's important to note that reverse engineering may have legal and ethical implications, and it should only be performed in controlled environments and with the necessary permissions and authorizations.

4.4 CODE ANALYSIS

Code analysis is a crucial aspect of static malware analysis that involves examining the code of a malware sample to understand its functionality, logic, and potential malicious behavior. By analyzing the code, analysts can uncover hidden or obfuscated functions, identify vulnerabilities, and gain insights into the malware's behavior and impact on a system. Here are the key steps involved in code analysis during malware analysis:

1. Code Structure and Organization:

   * Analyze the overall code structure: Study the organization of the code, such as the presence of modules, classes, functions, or subroutines. This analysis helps in understanding how the different parts of the malware interact with each other.

   * Identify entry points: Locate the main entry points of the code, which are responsible for initiating the malware's execution. This includes functions or routines that are called during program startup or through system hooks.

2. Function Analysis:

   * Identify key functions: Analyze functions or routines that handle critical operations, such as file manipulation, network communication, process injection, or encryption/ decryption. These functions often provide insights into the malware's primary functionalities and behavior.

   * Understand function interdependencies: Analyze how functions interact with each other, such as function calls, parameter passing, and return values. This helps in understanding the flow of data and control within the malware.

3. API Calls and System Interactions:

   * Identify system API calls: Determine the system calls made by the malware to interact with the underlying operating system. Analyzing these calls helps in understanding the malware's interactions with the system, such as file operations, network communication, or process manipulation.

   * Analyze API parameters and return values: Study the parameters passed to the API calls and the values returned by them. This analysis provides insights into the specific actions performed by the malware, such as file creation, registry modifications, or network connections.

4. Data Flow Analysis:

   * Track data flow: Trace the flow of critical data variables within the code to understand how they are processed,

modified, or used. This analysis helps in identifying the sources and destinations of data and understanding the data transformations performed by the malware.

✻ Identify data storage and encryption: Identify how and where the malware stores sensitive or malicious data. This includes analyzing data structures, buffers, or files used by the malware. Additionally, identify any encryption or obfuscation techniques used to hide data.

5. Control Flow Analysis:

✻ Understand program flow: Analyze the flow of the program by studying control structures, such as loops, conditional statements, and branching conditions. This analysis helps in understanding the decision-making logic and potential variations in the malware's behavior.

✻ Identify control flow hijacking: Look for any control flow hijacking techniques employed by the malware, such as code injection, hooking, or exploit-based attacks. This analysis helps in understanding how the malware gains control over the execution flow of legitimate programs.

6. Code Obfuscation and Anti-Analysis Techniques:

✻ Identify code obfuscation: Look for obfuscated or encrypted code designed to evade analysis. Analyze and deobfuscate the code to understand its true functionality.

✻ Handle anti-analysis tricks: Identify any anti-analysis techniques employed by the malware to hinder static analysis. These techniques may include code encryption, self-modifying code, junk code insertion, or control flow obfuscation. Reverse engineer and bypass these techniques to gain a clearer understanding of the code's behavior.

7. Vulnerability Identification:

✻ Identify code vulnerabilities: Analyze the code for potential security vulnerabilities, such as buffer overflows, input validation flaws, or insecure coding practices. Identifying vulnerabilities helps in understanding how the malware exploits these weaknesses to compromise a system.

Code analysis plays a vital role in understanding the inner workings of malware and is instrumental in developing effective detection and mitigation strategies. By analyzing the structure, functions, data flow, and control flow of the code, analysts can uncover the malware's intent, capabilities, and potential impact on a system.

4.5 DISASSEMBLERS AND DEBUGGERS

Disassemblers and debuggers are essential tools in the arsenal of a malware analyst during static analysis. They provide a deeper level of visibility into the inner workings of a malware sample, allowing analysts to understand the code execution, identify vulnerabilities, and uncover malicious behavior. Let's explore the role and functionality of disassemblers and debuggers in malware analysis:

1. Disassemblers:

   Disassemblers are tools that convert machine code (binary) into human-readable assembly code. They assist in the reverse engineering process by providing a low-level representation of the code. Here are some popular disassemblers used in malware analysis:

   * IDA Pro: IDA Pro is one of the most widely used disassemblers in the field of malware analysis. It offers a robust set of features, including advanced code analysis, interactive debugging, and plugin support.

   * radare2: radare2 is an open-source disassembler and debugger that provides a command-line interface for reverse engineering tasks. It supports a wide range of architectures and offers powerful analysis capabilities.

   * objdump: objdump is a command-line tool that is part of the GNU Binutils suite. It can disassemble executable files and object files, providing assembly code listings.

   Disassemblers allow analysts to examine the assembly instructions, control flow, and data flow within the malware's code. By studying the disassembled code, analysts can gain insights into the logic, functionality, and potential vulnerabilities present in the malware.

2. Debuggers:

Debuggers are tools that allow analysts to interactively execute and debug software, including malware samples. They provide features such as setting breakpoints, stepping through code, inspecting variables, and capturing runtime information. Debuggers play a crucial role in understanding the behavior and execution flow of malware. Here are some commonly used debuggers in malware analysis:

* OllyDbg: OllyDbg is a popular Windows debugger known for its user-friendly interface and powerful debugging capabilities. It allows analysts to step through the code, analyze registers and memory, and modify program behavior for analysis purposes.

* WinDbg: WinDbg is a debugger provided by Microsoft for Windows operating systems. It offers advanced debugging features and kernel-level debugging capabilities, making it suitable for analyzing malware at a deeper level.

* GDB: GDB (GNU Debugger) is a cross-platform debugger widely used in the Linux environment. It provides powerful debugging capabilities and supports various programming languages, making it useful for malware analysis on Linux-based systems.

Debuggers enable analysts to dynamically execute and monitor the behavior of malware samples. By stepping through the code and inspecting runtime data, analysts can understand how the malware interacts with the system, manipulate its behavior for analysis purposes, and identify specific malicious activities.

Disassemblers and debuggers are essential tools that assist malware analysts in unraveling the complexities of malware code. By using these tools effectively, analysts can gain a comprehensive understanding of the malware's behavior, identify its functionalities, and develop appropriate countermeasures to mitigate its impact.

Chapter 5

DYNAMIC MALWARE ANALYSIS

Dynamic malware analysis involves the execution of malware in a controlled environment to observe its behavior, gather runtime information, and understand its impact on a system. Unlike static analysis, which focuses on the analysis of the code or binary, dynamic analysis provides insights into the actual execution and runtime behavior of the malware. This approach is valuable for understanding how malware interacts with the system, its network communication, file modifications, and other malicious activities. Let's delve into the key aspects of dynamic malware analysis:

1. Execution Environment Setup:

    * Isolate the malware: Execute the malware in a controlled and isolated environment, such as a virtual machine (VM) or a sandbox. This prevents the malware from infecting the host system and allows for easy monitoring and analysis.

    * Network configuration: Configure the network settings of the execution environment to capture network traffic generated by the malware. This helps in understanding the malware's communication patterns, identifying command-and-control (C2) servers, and monitoring potential data exfiltration attempts.

2. Behavior Monitoring and Analysis:

    * System monitoring: Observe the system's behavior during malware execution, such as changes to the file system, registry, processes, and network connections. This analysis helps in identifying malicious activities, such as file drops,

registry modifications, process injections, or network communication.

✳ Dynamic analysis tools: Utilize dynamic analysis tools, such as process monitors, network traffic analyzers, and system activity monitors, to capture and analyze the runtime behavior of the malware. These tools provide real-time insights into the malware's actions and facilitate the identification of its capabilities.

✳ API call monitoring: Monitor the malware's interactions with system APIs by hooking or intercepting API calls. This allows for the identification of critical API calls and the parameters passed to them, shedding light on the malware's intentions and functionalities.

3. Malware Interaction and Response:

✳ Dynamic interaction: Interact with the malware during execution to trigger specific behaviors or gather additional information. This can include providing simulated inputs, modifying environment variables, or manipulating the execution flow to observe different code paths.

✳ Response analysis: Analyze the malware's response to interactions or environmental changes. This analysis helps in understanding how the malware adapts its behavior or reacts to certain stimuli, such as detecting virtual environments, evading analysis, or communicating with external entities.

4. Network Traffic Analysis:

✳ Capture and analyze network traffic: Monitor and capture network traffic generated by the malware. Analyze the network protocols, destinations, payloads, and communication patterns to identify C2 servers, data exfiltration attempts, or communication with other compromised systems.

✳ DNS analysis: Analyze DNS requests made by the malware to identify any communication with malicious domains or DNS-based evasion techniques employed by the malware.

5. Malware Payload Extraction:

    ✽   Extract and analyze payloads: If the malware downloads or drops additional payloads during execution, extract and analyze them separately. This allows for a deeper understanding of the complete attack chain, including potential secondary malware components or payload encryption techniques.

6. Dynamic Analysis Tools:

    ✽   Dynamic analysis frameworks: Utilize dynamic analysis frameworks, such as Cuckoo Sandbox, Joe Sandbox, or FireEye Sandbox, that provide automated and comprehensive analysis of malware samples. These frameworks often combine multiple dynamic analysis techniques, such as behavior monitoring, network traffic analysis, and memory analysis, to provide detailed insights into malware behavior.

    ✽   Debugger and code-level analysis: Employ debuggers, such as OllyDbg or WinDbg, during dynamic analysis to dynamically analyze and debug the malware's code execution. This allows for a granular examination of the code behavior, memory operations, and runtime modifications.

Dynamic malware analysis offers a practical approach to understanding the real-world behavior of malware and its impact on systems. By observing the malware's execution, monitoring its behavior, and analyzing the generated data, analysts can gain valuable insights into the malware's capabilities, intentions, and potential countermeasures.

5.1 DYNAMIC ANALYSIS SETUP

Setting up a proper dynamic analysis environment is crucial to effectively analyze malware and understand its behavior during execution. Here are the key steps involved in setting up a dynamic analysis environment:

1. Isolated Environment:

    ✽   Use a virtual machine (VM): Set up a dedicated VM for executing malware samples. This ensures isolation from the host system, preventing the malware from infecting or compromising the underlying system.

* Snapshot or clone VMs: Create a baseline snapshot or clone of the clean VM before executing any malware. This allows you to easily revert to a clean state for subsequent analyses.

2. Network Configuration:

* Bridged or NAT networking: Configure the VM's network settings to enable connectivity. You can choose between bridged networking, where the VM appears as a separate entity on the network, or NAT networking, where the VM shares the host system's network connection.

* Network monitoring: Set up network monitoring tools, such as Wireshark or tcpdump, to capture and analyze the network traffic generated by the malware. This helps in understanding the malware's communication patterns, identifying malicious domains or IP addresses, and detecting any data exfiltration attempts.

3. Malware Execution Environment:

* File execution: Copy the malware sample to the VM and execute it. Monitor the system's behavior during execution, including any changes to files, processes, registry entries, or network connections.

* Behavioral monitoring tools: Utilize dynamic analysis tools, such as Process Monitor, Process Explorer, or Sysinternals Suite, to monitor and capture the malware's behavior in real-time. These tools provide insights into the actions performed by the malware, such as file system modifications, registry changes, or process creations.

* Runtime analyzers: Employ runtime analysis tools, such as API monitors or behavior-based detectors, to capture the malware's interaction with system APIs. These tools help in identifying critical API calls, parameters passed, and the resulting actions taken by the malware.

4. Dynamic Interaction:

* Simulated input: Interact with the malware during execution by providing simulated inputs, such as fake

network responses, specific command-line arguments, or user input. This allows you to trigger specific behaviors or explore different code paths within the malware.

✱ Environmental manipulation: Modify the execution environment to simulate certain conditions or configurations that the malware may respond to. This can include altering environment variables, registry entries, or network settings.

5. Data and Memory Analysis:

✱ Data capture and analysis: Capture screenshots or video recordings of the malware's behavior during execution. This helps in documenting visual changes, GUI interactions, or any malicious activities that may not be captured by other monitoring tools.

✱ Memory analysis: Use memory analysis tools, such as Volatility or WinDbg, to analyze the runtime memory of the malware. This can reveal hidden processes, injected code, or decrypted payloads that may not be visible during static analysis.

6. Analysis Tools and Frameworks:

✱ Sandbox solutions: Consider using automated sandbox solutions, such as Cuckoo Sandbox, Joe Sandbox, or FireEye Sandbox, that provide comprehensive dynamic analysis capabilities. These frameworks automate the analysis process, including behavior monitoring, network traffic capture, and reporting of malware activities.

✱ Debuggers and emulators: Employ debuggers, such as OllyDbg or WinDbg, to dynamically analyze and debug the malware's code execution. This allows for in-depth examination of the code behavior, memory operations, and runtime modifications.

✱ Malware analysis platforms: Utilize commercial or open-source malware analysis platforms that offer integrated dynamic analysis capabilities. These platforms provide a centralized environment for executing malware, capturing dynamic data, and generating comprehensive analysis reports.

By following these steps and using the appropriate tools, you can establish an effective dynamic analysis environment to analyze malware samples and gain insights into their runtime behavior, interactions, and potential impact on systems.

5.2 BEHAVIORAL ANALYSIS

Behavioral analysis is a fundamental technique in dynamic malware analysis that focuses on observing and analyzing the actions and behaviors of malware during execution. By monitoring the malware's behavior in a controlled environment, analysts can gain valuable insights into its intentions, capabilities, and potential impact on a system. Here are the key steps involved in conducting behavioral analysis:

1. Execution Monitoring:

   * Environment setup: Execute the malware sample in an isolated environment, such as a virtual machine or sandbox, to ensure the safety of the host system.

   * Process monitoring: Utilize process monitoring tools, such as Process Monitor or Sysmon, to capture the system calls, file system activities, registry modifications, and network connections initiated by the malware. This provides a comprehensive view of the malware's interactions with the system.

2. Malicious Activities Identification:

   * File system analysis: Monitor changes to the file system, including file creations, modifications, and deletions. Pay attention to any suspicious file drops, unauthorized access attempts, or changes to critical system files.

   * Registry analysis: Observe modifications to the Windows registry, as malware often modifies registry entries to achieve persistence or evade detection. Identify any suspicious or unauthorized changes to registry keys and values.

   * Network traffic analysis: Capture and analyze network traffic generated by the malware. Look for outbound

connections, communication with known malicious IP addresses or domains, and data exfiltration attempts.

* Process behavior analysis: Monitor the behavior of the malware process, including the creation of child processes, code injections into legitimate processes, or any suspicious process termination attempts.

* System service and driver analysis: Analyze the installation and behavior of system services or drivers associated with the malware. Look for any unauthorized services or drivers, modifications to existing services, or attempts to escalate privileges.

3. Malware Interaction and Response:

* Dynamic interaction: Interact with the malware during execution by providing simulated inputs or altering the execution environment. This helps trigger specific behaviors, such as payload decryption, network communication, or evasion techniques.

* Response analysis: Analyze how the malware responds to interactions or environmental changes. Observe any adaptive behaviors, evasion tactics, or attempts to detect analysis environments.

4. Data Exfiltration and Command-and-Control (C2) Analysis:

* Network traffic capture: Analyze network traffic to identify communication with external entities, such as C2 servers. Look for patterns, protocols, or payloads that indicate data exfiltration, command retrieval, or other malicious activities.

* DNS analysis: Monitor DNS requests made by the malware to identify any communication with malicious domains or DNS-based evasion techniques.

5. Dynamic Analysis Tools:

* Sandboxing platforms: Utilize automated sandboxing platforms, such as Cuckoo Sandbox or Joe Sandbox, that provide behavioral analysis capabilities. These platforms

execute the malware sample in a controlled environment, capture behavioral data, and generate detailed reports.

✻ Network analysis tools: Employ network traffic analysis tools, such as Wireshark or Suricata, to capture and analyze the network traffic generated by the malware. These tools help in identifying communication patterns, protocols, and potential indicators of compromise.

6. Reporting and Analysis:

✻ Documentation: Document the observed behaviors, activities, and interactions of the malware during dynamic analysis. This includes recording timestamps, file modifications, network connections, and any other relevant information.

✻ Behavior-based indicators: Extract behavior-based indicators, such as registry modifications, file system activities, or network communication patterns, that can be used to detect similar malware in the future.

✻ Analysis correlation: Combine behavioral analysis findings with other analysis techniques, such as static analysis or code-level analysis, to gain a comprehensive understanding of the malware's capabilities and impact.

Behavioral analysis provides crucial insights into the actions and behaviors of malware, helping analysts understand its functionality, potential risks, and countermeasures. By carefully monitoring and analyzing the malware's behavior, analysts can strengthen their defense strategies and mitigate the impact of malicious software.

5.3 NETWORK TRAFFIC ANALYSIS

Network traffic analysis is a vital component of dynamic malware analysis that focuses on monitoring and analyzing the network communication generated by malware during execution. By capturing and examining the network traffic, analysts can gain valuable insights into the malware's communication patterns, command-and-control (C2) infrastructure, data exfiltration attempts, and potential network-based indicators of compromise. Here are the key steps involved in network traffic analysis during dynamic malware analysis:

1. Network Traffic Capture:

   * Network monitoring setup: Set up a network monitoring tool, such as Wireshark, tcpdump, or Suricata, to capture the network traffic generated by the malware during execution.

   * Virtual machine or sandbox configuration: Configure the network settings of the execution environment, such as the network adapter and IP configuration, to enable network connectivity for the malware.

   * Traffic capture filters: Apply appropriate filters to capture only the relevant network traffic associated with the malware. These filters can include specific IP addresses, ports, protocols, or traffic patterns of interest.

2. Analysis of Network Protocols:

   * Protocol identification: Identify the network protocols used by the malware, such as HTTP, DNS, FTP, or IRC. This helps in understanding the communication channels and their associated behaviors.

   * Protocol decoding: Analyze the captured network traffic and decode the network protocols to extract relevant information, such as HTTP headers, DNS queries, or FTP commands. This provides insights into the malware's communication mechanisms and potential malicious activities.

3. Command-and-Control (C2) Analysis:

   * C2 communication identification: Look for network connections or traffic patterns indicative of command-and-control communication. These may include outbound connections to specific IP addresses, unusual port numbers, or non-standard protocols.

   * C2 infrastructure mapping: Analyze the network traffic to identify the IP addresses, domain names, or URLs associated with the malware's command-and-control infrastructure. This information is crucial for threat intelligence, as it can help identify other infected systems or malicious servers.

✳ C2 communication patterns: Observe the frequency, timing, and content of the network communication between the malware and its C2 server. This analysis provides insights into the malware's command retrieval, data exfiltration, or update mechanisms.

4. Data Exfiltration Analysis:

✳ Payload inspection: Inspect the captured network traffic for any data payloads transmitted by the malware. This may include sensitive information, stolen credentials, or exfiltrated files.

✳ Encryption and encoding analysis: Determine if the malware employs any encryption or encoding techniques to obfuscate the exfiltrated data. Decrypting or decoding these payloads can reveal their contents and shed light on the stolen information.

5. Network Indicators of Compromise (IOCs):

✳ IOC extraction: Extract potential indicators of compromise from the network traffic, such as IP addresses, domain names, URLs, or unique traffic patterns. These IOCs can be used to detect similar malware infections in other environments.

✳ IOC correlation: Cross-reference the extracted IOCs with threat intelligence feeds, known malicious domains, or IP reputation databases to identify known malicious infrastructure or previously documented malware campaigns.

6. Reporting and Analysis:

✳ Documentation: Record and document the observed network traffic, including timestamps, source/destination IP addresses, protocols used, and any other relevant information.

✳ Visualization: Utilize network traffic visualization tools, such as Wireshark's packet plotting feature or flow-based visualizations, to gain a visual understanding of the network traffic patterns and communication flows.

✳ Analysis correlation: Combine the network traffic analysis findings with other analysis techniques, such as behavioral analysis or code-level analysis, to obtain a comprehensive understanding of the malware's behavior and impact.

Network traffic analysis provides critical insights into the malware's communication infrastructure, data exfiltration attempts, and potential indicators of compromise. By analyzing the network traffic generated by malware during dynamic analysis, analysts can strengthen their defense mechanisms and develop effective countermeasures against network-based threats.

5.4 API MONITORING

API (Application Programming Interface) monitoring is a key aspect of dynamic malware analysis that involves observing and analyzing the interactions between the malware and the operating system's APIs during execution. By monitoring the API calls made by the malware, analysts can gain insights into its functionality, system interactions, and potential malicious activities. Here are the key steps involved in API monitoring during dynamic malware analysis:

1. API Monitoring Setup:

   ✳ Dynamic analysis environment: Set up a controlled environment, such as a virtual machine or sandbox, to execute the malware and monitor its API calls.

   ✳ Monitoring tools: Utilize API monitoring tools or frameworks, such as Process Monitor, API Monitor, or Sysmon, to capture and log the API calls made by the malware.

2. API Call Capture and Analysis:

   ✳ API call capture: Monitor and log the API calls invoked by the malware during execution. These calls include functions related to file operations, registry access, network communication, process manipulation, and more.

   ✳ API call analysis: Analyze the captured API calls to understand the malware's interactions with the operating system and the actions it performs. Pay attention to suspicious or unauthorized API calls that may indicate malicious behavior.

3. Behavior Identification and Analysis:

*   File system operations: Monitor and analyze the malware's file-related API calls, such as file creation, modification, deletion, or access. Identify any unauthorized file operations or attempts to modify critical system files.

*   Registry interactions: Observe the malware's registry-related API calls to detect any modifications to the system registry. Look for unauthorized changes, creation of new registry entries, or attempts to hide its presence.

*   Network-related API calls: Analyze the network-related API calls made by the malware to identify communication with external entities, such as HTTP requests, socket operations, or DNS queries. Look for suspicious network activities, communication with known malicious IP addresses or domains, or data exfiltration attempts.

*   Process manipulation: Monitor API calls related to process creation, termination, injection, or manipulation. Identify any suspicious process behaviors, such as injecting code into legitimate processes or terminating security-related processes.

*   Privilege escalation attempts: Analyze API calls related to privilege escalation, such as accessing sensitive system resources, bypassing security mechanisms, or altering user privileges. Look for attempts to gain elevated privileges or escalate its access level.

4. Dynamic Interaction:

*   Simulated input: Interact with the malware during execution by providing simulated inputs or altering the execution environment. This helps trigger specific behaviors or explore different code paths within the malware.

*   Environmental manipulation: Modify the execution environment or system parameters to simulate certain

conditions or configurations that the malware may respond to. This can include altering environment variables, registry entries, or network settings.

5. Analysis Tools and Frameworks:

    ✷ API monitoring frameworks: Utilize specialized API monitoring frameworks, such as Cuckoo Sandbox, to automate the monitoring and analysis of API calls. These frameworks provide detailed reports, behavior logs, and insights into the malware's API interactions.

    ✷ Dynamic analysis platforms: Consider using commercial or open-source dynamic analysis platforms that offer integrated API monitoring capabilities. These platforms provide a centralized environment for executing malware, capturing API data, and generating comprehensive analysis reports.

6. Reporting and Analysis:

    ✷ Documentation: Record and document the observed API calls, including the function names, parameters, return values, and any relevant context.

    ✷ Behavior-based indicators: Extract behavior-based indicators from the API calls, such as specific function sequences, parameter values, or unique API patterns, that can be used to detect similar malware in the future.

    ✷ Analysis correlation: Combine the API monitoring findings with other analysis techniques, such as behavioral analysis, network traffic analysis, or code-level analysis, to obtain a comprehensive understanding of the malware's capabilities and impact.

API monitoring provides valuable insights into the malware's system interactions, functionalities, and potential malicious activities during dynamic analysis. By analyzing the API calls made by the malware, analysts can uncover its behavior patterns, detect malicious actions, and develop effective countermeasures to protect against API-based threats.

5.5 SYSTEM MONITORING

System monitoring is a critical component of dynamic malware analysis that involves observing and analyzing the behavior of a malware sample as it interacts with the underlying operating system. By monitoring various system-level activities, analysts can gain insights into the malware's impact on the system, its attempts to evade detection, and potential vulnerabilities it exploits. Here are the key aspects of system monitoring during dynamic malware analysis:

1. Process Monitoring:

   * Process execution: Monitor the creation and termination of processes by the malware. Pay attention to any suspicious or unauthorized processes spawned by the malware, as well as its interaction with existing processes.

   * Process behavior: Analyze the behavior of the malware's processes, such as code injection into legitimate processes, modification of process memory, or attempts to manipulate process privileges.

   * Process enumeration: Enumerate the running processes and analyze their relationships to identify any anomalous or malicious activities.

2. Memory Analysis:

   * Memory modifications: Monitor changes made by the malware to process memory, such as code injections, hooking techniques, or modifications to critical system data structures.

   * Malicious payloads: Identify any payloads or data structures injected into memory by the malware. Analyze the content, purpose, and execution flow of these payloads to understand the malware's intentions.

   * Heap and stack analysis: Scrutinize the heap and stack memory regions for any abnormal behavior, such as buffer overflows, heap corruptions, or stack manipulations, which could indicate the presence of malware.

3. Registry Monitoring:

    *   Registry modifications: Monitor changes made by the malware to the Windows registry. Identify any suspicious or unauthorized modifications to registry keys and values, as malware often leverages the registry for persistence or configuration.

    *   Startup entries: Track changes in registry entries related to system startup, such as modifications to "Run" or "RunOnce" keys. These changes may indicate attempts by the malware to achieve persistence.

4. File System Monitoring:

    *   File operations: Monitor the malware's interactions with the file system, including file creations, modifications, and deletions. Pay attention to any suspicious file drops, unauthorized access attempts, or modifications to critical system files.

    *   File analysis: Analyze the content and structure of files dropped or modified by the malware. This analysis helps identify potential payloads, configuration files, or encrypted data.

5. Network Activity Monitoring:

    *   Network connections: Monitor the malware's network connections, including outbound connections, communication with specific IP addresses or domains, and data transfer. Identify any suspicious network activity, such as communication with known malicious entities or unexpected data exfiltration attempts.

    *   Network protocol analysis: Analyze the network protocols used by the malware, such as HTTP, DNS, or IRC, to understand its communication mechanisms and potential command-and-control (C2) infrastructure.

6. System Events and Logs:

    *   Event log analysis: Analyze system event logs, such as Windows Event Viewer, to identify any security-related

events triggered by the malware. Look for entries related to process creation, registry modifications, network connections, or system service changes.

* Security auditing: Enable security auditing mechanisms to log specific system events and actions performed by the malware. This helps in capturing and analyzing detailed information about the malware's activities.

7. Analysis Tools and Frameworks:

* Endpoint security solutions: Utilize endpoint security solutions that provide real-time monitoring and analysis of system activities. These solutions can detect and alert on suspicious behaviors, potential malware activity, or system anomalies.

* Host-based intrusion detection systems (HIDS): Deploy HIDS tools that monitor system events, file integrity, and process behavior to detect potential intrusions or unauthorized activities.

* Event log analysis tools: Utilize event log analysis tools, such as Splunk, ELK Stack, or Windows

Event Forwarding, to aggregate and analyze system logs for potential indicators of compromise (IOCs).

System monitoring provides crucial insights into the malware's impact on the system, its evasion techniques, and potential vulnerabilities it exploits. By analyzing the behavior and activities observed during system monitoring, analysts can develop effective mitigation strategies, detect future malware infections, and enhance overall system security.

Chapter 6

MALWARE DEOBFUSCATION AND DECRYPTION

Malware authors often employ various obfuscation and encryption techniques to evade detection and make analysis more challenging. Deobfuscation and decryption techniques play a crucial role in malware analysis as they help uncover the hidden functionalities, reveal the actual code structure, and enable further analysis. Here are some common techniques used for malware deobfuscation and decryption:

1. String Deobfuscation:

    * Character encoding: Malware may use different character encodings, such as Base64, XOR, or custom algorithms, to obfuscate strings. Reverse-engineering these encodings and applying appropriate decoding algorithms can reveal the original strings.

    * String manipulation: Malware may perform various string manipulation operations, such as splitting, concatenation, or bitwise operations, to obscure strings. Analyzing these operations and reversing them can reconstruct the original strings.

2. Code Deobfuscation:

    * Control flow analysis: Malware may use obfuscated control flow techniques, such as junk code insertion, dead code, or opaque predicates, to confuse analysis tools and analysts. Understanding the legitimate control flow and identifying and removing the obfuscated code paths can reveal the true execution flow.

* Anti-debugging techniques: Malware may employ anti-debugging tricks, such as debugger checks, timing-based checks, or environment checks, to hinder analysis. Bypassing or circumventing these anti-debugging techniques can allow for effective analysis of the malware.

* Virtualization and packers: Malware authors may use packers or virtualization techniques to obfuscate the code and make it more difficult to analyze. Unpacking or de-virtualizing the code reveals the original executable, enabling further analysis.

3. Encryption and Decryption:

* Encrypted payloads: Malware may encrypt sensitive payloads, configuration files, or communication channels to protect them from analysis and detection. Identifying the encryption algorithms and keys, and applying appropriate decryption techniques, can unveil the hidden content.

* Memory decryption: Some malware encrypts critical portions of its code or payload in memory to evade static analysis. Analyzing the memory regions, identifying the decryption routines, and decrypting the content in memory can expose the actual code or payload.

4. Runtime Analysis:

* Debugger and dynamic analysis: Running the malware in a controlled environment with a debugger or dynamic analysis tool allows for monitoring the runtime behavior, including memory modifications, API calls, and network interactions. Observing the malware's behavior during execution can provide insights into its deobfuscation or decryption routines.

* Dynamic memory analysis: Monitoring the memory state during runtime can help identify dynamically generated or decrypted code. Examining memory regions, identifying self-modifying code, and capturing decrypted content can aid in understanding the malware's true functionality.

5. Automated Tools and Techniques:

   * Static analysis tools: Leveraging automated tools, such as disassemblers, deobfuscators, or code analysis frameworks, can assist in automated deobfuscation and decryption of the malware. These tools apply various algorithms and techniques to identify and remove obfuscation layers.

   * Scripting and programming languages: Writing custom scripts or programs using languages like Python or PowerShell can automate deobfuscation or decryption tasks. These scripts can implement known algorithms or techniques specific to the malware under analysis.

6. Collaborative Research and Threat Intelligence:

   * Knowledge sharing: Collaborating with the security community, participating in forums, and sharing findings with fellow analysts can provide insights and collective knowledge on deobfuscation and decryption techniques for specific malware families or trends.

   * Threat intelligence feeds: Leveraging threat intelligence platforms and feeds can provide valuable information on known obfuscation and decryption techniques used by prevalent malware. This knowledge can aid in effectively deobfuscating or decrypting similarsamples.

Malware deobfuscation and decryption are crucial steps in the analysis process to reveal the true nature of the malware and understand its behavior and capabilities. By employing various techniques, tools, and collaboration with the security community, analysts can effectively reverse-engineer obfuscated and encrypted malware to gain valuable insights for mitigation and protection measures.

6.1 COMMON OBFUSCATION TECHNIQUES

Malware authors employ a variety of obfuscation techniques to complicate the analysis process and evade detection by security solutions. These techniques aim to conceal the true intent and functionality of the malware, making it challenging for analysts to understand its behavior. Here are some common obfuscation techniques used by malware authors:

1. Code Obfuscation:

   * Variable and function renaming: Malware authors often rename variables and functions with meaningless or random names to make the code difficult to understand. This makes it harder for analysts to decipher the purpose and flow of the code.

   * Dead code insertion: Malware may contain sections of code that serve no functional purpose other than to confuse analysis tools and analysts. These sections may include unused functions, unreachable code branches, or code that is conditionally executed but never triggered during normal execution.

   * Code packing and compression: Malware may be packed or compressed using specialized tools to make the code unreadable and increase its size. Packers and compressors can encrypt the code, modify its structure, or add additional layers of obfuscation to hinder analysis.

   * Anti-analysis checks: Malware can include checks to detect the presence of analysis tools, virtual environments, or debuggers. If these checks detect analysis attempts, the malware may alter its behavior or terminate execution, making analysis more difficult.

2. String Obfuscation:

   * String encryption: Malware often encrypts sensitive strings, such as URLs, command-and-control (C2) server addresses, or configuration data, to prevent easy identification. The strings are encrypted using algorithms or custom encryption schemes, requiring decryption at runtime.

   * String splitting: Malware may split strings into multiple parts and store them in different locations in the code. These parts are then concatenated and decrypted at runtime, making it harder to identify and analyze the complete string.

   * ASCII or Unicode encoding: Malware authors may use ASCII or Unicode encoding to obfuscate strings. This involves converting each character to its ASCII or Unicode representation, making the strings less recognizable.

3. Control Flow Obfuscation:

    *   Opaque predicates: Malware may use conditional statements with complex logic and redundant code branches to confuse static analysis tools. These opaque predicates create multiple possible code paths, making it difficult to determine the actual execution flow.

    *   Code flattening: Malware authors can flatten the code by converting structured constructs, such as loops and conditionals, into a single block of code. This makes it challenging to understand the logical flow of the program and identify important control flow structures.

    *   Jump-oriented programming (JOP) and return-oriented programming (ROP): Advanced malware can leverage JOP or ROP techniques to construct malicious code paths using existing code fragments (gadgets) within the target application. This technique avoids the need to inject additional code, making it harder to detect and analyze.

4. Data Obfuscation:

    *   Data encoding: Malware may encode or transform data to hide its true nature. This can involve using encoding schemes like Base64, XOR, or custom algorithms to obfuscate sensitive data such as configuration files, command parameters, or payloads.

    *   File format manipulation: Malware can manipulate file formats, such as modifying header information or embedding encrypted data within benign files. This helps the malware evade detection and analysis by security solutions that rely on file signatures or known file formats.

5. Anti-Debugging Techniques:

    *   Debugger detection: Malware can employ techniques to detect the presence of a debugger, such as checking for specific registry keys, examining debug flags, or monitoring system processes. If a debugger is detected, the malware may alter its behavior or terminate execution to evade analysis.

✳ Timing-based checks: Malware may introduce timing delays or execute code based on specific timing conditions. These techniques make it difficult to debug the malware's behavior accurately, as the timing-dependent code may behave differently in a controlled environment.

These obfuscation techniques aim to make the analysis process more challenging by complicating code understanding, data extraction, and execution flow identification. Analysts need to employ various deobfuscation and analysis techniques to uncover the true nature of the malware and understand its behavior and potential impact.

6.2 UNPACKING AND DECRYPTION

Malware authors often employ packing and encryption techniques to obfuscate their code and evade detection by security solutions. Unpacking and decrypting the malware is a critical step in the analysis process, as it reveals the original code and enables further analysis. Here are common techniques used for unpacking and decrypting malware:

1. Static Unpacking:

   ✳ Identify the packer: Analyze the malware to determine the type of packer used. This can involve examining the file structure, headers, or specific packer signatures.

   ✳ Signature-based unpacking: Use known signatures or patterns associated with the packer to identify and extract the packed sections of the malware. Tools like UPX, PEiD, or YARA rules can assist in this process.

   ✳ Unpacking tools: Utilize specialized unpacking tools designed to automatically unpack common packers. These tools can extract the original code and restore it to its unpacked form.

   ✳ Manual unpacking: In cases where automated tools fail, manual unpacking techniques may be required. This involves understanding the packer's structure, identifying the decryption routine, and manually extracting the original code.

2. Runtime Unpacking:

    *   Dynamic analysis: Execute the packed malware in a controlled environment and monitor its behavior using a debugger or dynamic analysis tool. Analyze the runtime activities, such as memory modifications or code execution, to identify the unpacking routine.

    *   Memory dumping: Capture the memory state during runtime analysis and extract the unpacked code from the memory dump. Tools like Volatility or WinDbg can assist in memory analysis and extraction.

    *   Hooking techniques: Malware may use hooking techniques to intercept and modify system functions or APIs. Identifying and bypassing these hooks can reveal the unpacked code and facilitate further analysis.

3. Decryption:

    *   Identify encryption algorithms: Analyze the malware to determine the encryption algorithms used. This can involve examining the encryption routines, identifying specific instructions or algorithms, or searching for encryption-related strings or constants.

    *   Static decryption: Reverse-engineer the encryption routine to understand the encryption process and extract the decryption key or algorithm. This can involve analyzing the sequence of operations, reverse-engineering the encryption algorithm, or identifying key generation routines.

    *   Dynamic decryption: Execute the malware in a controlled environment and monitor the decryption process during runtime analysis. Capture the decrypted content or observe the memory modifications to recover the original code or data.

    *   Emulation and sandboxing: Utilize emulation or sandboxing tools that simulate the malware's execution environment. These tools can intercept and capture the decrypted content as it is being executed.

4. Anti-Analysis Techniques:

   * Anti-unpacking mechanisms: Malware may employ anti-unpacking techniques to detect and thwart unpacking attempts. These techniques can include checksum verifications, integrity checks, or code modifications that alter the unpacking process. Analyzing and bypassing these techniques may be necessary to successfully unpack the malware.

   * Anti-debugging measures: Malware can implement anti-debugging techniques to hinder analysis. These techniques can include checks for debug flags, debugger presence, or system-level hooks. Bypassing or circumventing these anti-debugging measures may be required to successfully unpack the malware.

Unpacking and decrypting malware allows analysts to gain access to the original code, revealing the true behavior and capabilities of the malicious software. This step is crucial for conducting further analysis, understanding the malware's functionality, and developing appropriate mitigation strategies.

6.3 CODE RECONSTRUCTION

During the malware analysis process, code reconstruction is an essential step in understanding the functionality, logic, and behavior of the malware. Code reconstruction involves reverse-engineering the malware's disassembled or decompiled code to reconstruct a higher-level representation that is easier to analyze. Here are common techniques used for code reconstruction:

1. Disassembly and Decompilation:

   * Disassembly: Convert the machine code of the malware into assembly language instructions using disassemblers like IDA Pro, Radare2, or Binary Ninja. This provides a low-level representation of the code, making it easier to understand the instructions and control flow.

   * Decompilation: Transform the disassembled code into a higher-level programming language representation, such as C or C++, using decompilers like Ghidra, RetDec, or

Hex-Rays. Decompilers attempt to recover the original source code structure, variables, and control flow from the assembly code.

2. Control Flow Reconstruction:

    *   Control flow analysis: Analyze the disassembled code to identify the sequence of instructions, loops, conditionals, and function calls. This helps reconstruct the control flow graph of the malware, allowing for a better understanding of the logic and execution paths.

    *   Identifying functions: Identify and name functions within the code to better organize and comprehend the different components of the malware.

    *   Control flow graph generation: Use tools like IDA Pro, Ghidra, or Angr to generate visual representations of the control flow graph, making it easier to analyze the malware's behavior.

3. Variable and Data Analysis:

    *   Variable identification: Analyze the disassembled code to identify and name variables used by the malware. This helps in understanding the purpose and usage of specific data within the code.

    *   Data structure reconstruction: Determine the structure and organization of complex data objects, such as data buffers or data structures, used by the malware. This helps in understanding the data flow and interactions within the malware.

    *   Data type inference: Infer the data types of variables and parameters used by the malware, which aids in understanding the purpose and usage of specific data elements.

4. Code Annotation and Documentation:

    *   Commenting and documentation: Add comments, annotations, and documentation to the disassembled or decompiled code to describe the functionality, purpose,

and behavior of specific code segments. This helps in documenting the analysis findings and facilitates knowledge sharing among analysts.

✻ Naming conventions: Use meaningful names for functions, variables, and other code elements to enhance code readability and comprehension. This makes it easier for analysts to understand the code during subsequent analysis or when collaborating with others.

5. Control Flow Simplification:

✻ Code optimization: Simplify the disassembled or decompiled code by removing unnecessary instructions, dead code, or redundant code segments. This helps in reducing code complexity and focusing on the essential parts of the malware.

✻ Code restructuring: Rearrange the code segments to improve readability and facilitate code comprehension. This can involve reordering instructions, grouping related instructions together, or splitting code into separate functions or subroutines.

Code reconstruction plays a vital role in understanding the inner workings of the malware, identifying key functionalities, and analyzing its behavior. It enables analysts to gain insights into the malware's logic, identify potential vulnerabilities or exploits, and develop effective countermeasures and mitigation strategies.

6.4 IDENTIFYING PERSISTENCE MECHANISMS

Persistence mechanisms are techniques used by malware to maintain their presence on an infected system even after a reboot or system restart. Identifying these persistence mechanisms is crucial for understanding how the malware maintains its foothold and ensuring effective removal. Here are common techniques used to identify persistence mechanisms in malware:

1. Startup Locations:

✻ Registry Keys: Malware often creates or modifies registry keys to ensure it is executed during system startup. Analyze common startup registry keys such as "Run," "RunOnce," or "RunServices" in both the current user and local machine hives.

- Startup Folders: Malware may drop itself or create shortcuts in the user's startup folder to achieve persistence. Check the common startup folders like "%AppData%\Microsoft\Windows\Start Menu\Programs\Startup" for any suspicious files or shortcuts.
- Scheduled Tasks: Malware can create scheduled tasks to execute at specific times or events. Examine the Windows Task Scheduler for any unusual or suspicious tasks that may indicate malware persistence.

2. System Services:
   - Windows Services: Malware may install itself as a Windows service to achieve persistence. Analyze the list of installed services, their properties, and associated binaries for any suspicious entries.
   - Service DLL Hijacking: Malware can exploit vulnerable or misconfigured services by replacing legitimate service DLLs with malicious ones. Identify services that load external DLLs and verify the integrity and authenticity of the loaded DLLs.
3. Boot Sector and Master Boot Record (MBR):
   - Bootkits: Sophisticated malware may infect the boot sector or MBR to gain persistence and execute before the operating system loads. Analyze the boot sector and MBR for any modifications or signs of infection using specialized tools or forensic techniques.
4. Autorun and AutoPlay:
   - Removable Media: Malware can leverage autorun or autoplay features to execute automatically when removable media, such as USB drives or CDs, are connected to the system. Disable autorun or autoplay features and scan removable media for suspicious files or autorun.inf files.

5. Browser Extensions and Plugins:

   ✻ Browser Hijackers: Some malware achieves persistence by installing malicious browser extensions or plugins. Check the installed browser extensions and plugins for any suspicious or unknown entries.

   ✻ Browser Settings: Malware may modify browser settings, such as the default homepage, search engine, or proxy settings, to redirect or control user web traffic. Review the browser settings for any unauthorized changes.

6. Windows Startup Programs:

   ✻ Startup Applications: Analyze the list of programs configured to run at system startup. Check the "Startup" folder, the "msconfig" utility, or third-party startup management tools to identify any suspicious entries.

7. Other Persistence Mechanisms:

   ✻ COM Objects and Registry Keys: Malware may register itself as a COM object or create specific registry keys to achieve persistence. Monitor the COM object registrations and analyze the registry for any suspicious entries.

   ✻ Kernel-mode Rootkits: Advanced malware may use kernel-level techniques to hide and maintain persistence on the system. Conduct deep analysis using specialized tools and techniques to identify such rootkits.

To identify persistence mechanisms effectively, employ a combination of manual analysis techniques, system monitoring tools, and security solutions. Regularly update and scan systems for malware, keep software and operating systems patched, and maintain a strong security posture to prevent and detect persistent malware infections.

Chapter 7

MALWARE REVERSE ENGINEERING

Malware reverse engineering is the process of analyzing malicious software to understand its inner workings, behavior, and capabilities. By reverse engineering malware, analysts can uncover important information about its functionality, identify potential vulnerabilities, and develop effective countermeasures. Here are the key steps involved in malware reverse engineering:

1. Obtaining the Malware Sample:

    *   Acquire the malware sample: Obtain a copy of the malware that you want to analyze. This can be done by capturing it from an infected system, downloading it from a reliable malware repository, or receiving it from a trusted source.

2. Malware Analysis Environment:

    *   Set up a controlled environment: Create a secure and isolated environment for analyzing the malware. Use virtual machines, sandboxing tools, or dedicated analysis systems to prevent the malware from infecting other systems or compromising sensitive data.

3. Static Analysis:

    *   File analysis: Begin by examining the malware's file structure, headers, and metadata. Identify file type, file format, and any additional files or resources associated with the malware.

    *   Strings and metadata examination: Extract strings and metadata embedded in the malware to gain insights into

its functionality, authorship, and potential indicators of compromise (IOCs).

✳ Code analysis: Disassemble or decompile the malware to understand its low-level instructions, control flow, and data structures. Use tools like IDA Pro, Ghidra, or radare2 to assist in the disassembly or decompilation process.

✳ API analysis: Identify the application programming interfaces (APIs) called by the malware to interact with the operating system, network, or other software components. Analyzing the API calls can reveal the malware's capabilities and provide insights into its behavior.

4. Dynamic Analysis:

✳ Behavioral analysis: Execute the malware in a controlled environment while monitoring its behavior. Use tools like debuggers, emulators, or virtual machines to observe system-level interactions, network communications, file modifications, and registry changes.

✳ Network traffic analysis: Capture and analyze network traffic generated by the malware. This can help identify command-and-control (C&C) servers, communication protocols, and data exfiltration methods.

✳ Memory analysis: Capture the memory state during runtime analysis to identify in-memory artifacts, such as injected code, process hollowing, or DLL injections. Tools like Volatility or WinDbg can assist in memory forensics and analysis.

5. Code Reconstruction:

✳ Reconstruct the high-level representation: Reverse-engineer the disassembled code to reconstruct a higher-level representation, such as pseudo-code or a programming language-like structure. This makes it easier to understand the malware's logic, functions, and control flow.

6. Malicious Functionality Analysis:

✳ Analyze specific functionality: Focus on analyzing the critical functionalities of the malware, such as data exfiltration, privilege escalation, persistence mechanisms, anti-analysis techniques, or payload delivery methods. This analysis helps in understanding the potential impact of the malware and developing appropriate countermeasures.

7. Indicators of Compromise (IOCs):

    *   Extract IOCs: Identify IOCs, such as file names, file paths, registry keys, network signatures, or behavior patterns, that can be used to detect and mitigate the presence of the malware in other systems or networks.

8. Reporting and Documentation:

    *   Document findings: Document the analysis process, observations, findings, and conclusions. This documentation serves as a reference for future analysis, collaboration with other analysts, or for legal and forensic purposes.

Throughout the reverse engineering process, it's important to adhere to legal and ethical considerations, respect intellectual property rights, and ensure that the analysis environment remains secure to prevent accidental malware propagation or exposure.

7.1 DISASSEMBLING AND DECOMPILING

Disassembling and decompiling are fundamental techniques in malware reverse engineering that allow analysts to convert machine code into a more human-readable form. These processes provide insight into the functionality, logic, and behavior of the malware. Here's an overview of disassembling and decompiling in malware analysis:

Disassembling:

Disassembling is the process of converting machine code, typically in the form of binary executable files, into assembly language instructions. Assembly language is a low-level programming language that is closely tied to the architecture and instruction set of the target processor. Disassembling allows analysts to examine the instructions and control flow of the malware. The following are common tools used for disassembling:

1. IDA Pro: IDA Pro is a widely used disassembler that supports multiple architectures and provides a comprehensive set of analysis and debugging features. It allows analysts to navigate through the disassembled code, visualize control flow graphs, and annotate the code with comments and labels.

2. Ghidra: Ghidra is a free and open-source disassembler developed by the National Security Agency (NSA). It offers features similar to IDA Pro, including code navigation, cross-references, and scripting capabilities.

3. Radare2: Radare2 is a command-line disassembler and debugger known for its versatility and extensibility. It supports various architectures and provides a rich set of features for code analysis and manipulation.

Decompiling:

Decompiling is the process of converting machine code back into a higher-level programming language representation, such as C or C++. Decompiling allows analysts to understand the functionality of the malware at a higher level of abstraction, resembling the original source code. Although decompilers can provide valuable insights, it's important to note that decompiled code may not always be 100% accurate or easily readable, especially in the case of obfuscated or heavily optimized code. The following are common tools used for decompiling:

1. Hex-Rays IDA with Hex-Rays Decompiler: IDA Pro, when equipped with the Hex-Rays Decompiler plugin, can decompile x86 and ARM code into a higher-level representation. The Hex-Rays Decompiler attempts to recover the original C code structure, making it easier to understand the malware's logic and functionality.

2. RetDec: RetDec is an open-source decompiler that supports a wide range of architectures. It aims to provide a robust decompilation process and offers a web-based interface along with a command-line version.

3. Ghidra: As mentioned earlier, Ghidra not only supports disassembling but also provides a decompiler module. Analysts can utilize this feature to decompile the disassembled code and obtain a higher-level representation.

It's worth noting that disassembling and decompiling are complementary techniques, and both can be used in combination during malware analysis. Disassembling helps in understanding the low-level instructions and control flow, while decompiling provides a higher-level understanding of the malware's functionality. The choice between disassembling and decompiling depends on the specific requirements of the analysis and the capabilities of the available tools.

7.2 ANALYZING ASSEMBLY CODE

Analyzing assembly code is a crucial aspect of malware reverse engineering. Assembly code provides a low-level representation of the malware's instructions and control flow, allowing analysts to understand its behavior, functionality, and potential vulnerabilities. Here are some key techniques and considerations for analyzing assembly code in the context of malware analysis:

1. Code Structure and Control Flow:

   * Identify entry points: Determine the entry points of the malware by locating the main function or the initial code block. This helps in understanding where the execution begins and how the control flow is established.

   * Trace execution flow: Follow the execution flow by analyzing branches, loops, and function calls. Identify conditional and unconditional jumps, loops, and function calls to understand how the malware makes decisions and interacts with different parts of the code.

2. Function Analysis:

   * Identify function boundaries: Identify the boundaries of functions within the assembly code. Look for function prologues (e.g., push ebp; mov ebp, esp) and epilogues (e.g., mov esp, ebp; pop ebp) to identify the start and end of functions.

   * Parameter passing: Observe how function parameters are passed and accessed within the assembly code. Identify the calling conventions used (e.g., cdecl, stdcall) and the corresponding stack manipulation.

✻   Function behavior: Analyze the instructions within each function to understand its purpose, such as file manipulation, network communication, or encryption/decryption routines.

3. Instruction Analysis:

✻   Opcode analysis: Understand the meaning and functionality of different opcodes and their operands. Reference architecture-specific documentation and manuals to gain familiarity with the instruction set.

✻   Memory manipulation: Observe how memory is accessed, read, and written within the code. Identify any buffer overflows, heap/stack manipulations, or other memory-related vulnerabilities.

✻   String analysis: Look for string constants and analyze how they are used within the code. Strings can reveal important information such as file names, registry keys, or network addresses.

✻   System calls and API usage: Identify system calls or API functions used by the malware to interact with the operating system or external libraries. Understand the purpose and potential impact of these calls.

4. Data Analysis:

✻   Data types and structures: Identify and analyze data types, structures, and constants used within the assembly code. This includes identifying strings, integers, arrays, or pointers.

✻   Variable and register usage: Keep track of how registers and memory locations are used to store and manipulate data. Determine which values represent variables, constants, or temporary calculations.

5. Code Obfuscation and Anti-Analysis Techniques:

✻   Obfuscated code: Look for obfuscation techniques employed by the malware to complicate analysis, such as code encryption, junk code insertion, or control flow obfuscation. Try to identify and understand the purpose of the obfuscated sections.

* Anti-analysis tricks: Watch out for anti-analysis techniques used by the malware to evade detection or hinder analysis, such as anti-debugging checks, time-based triggers, or code self-modification. Recognize and overcome these techniques to fully understand the malware's behavior.

6. Code Documentation and Annotation:

* Commenting and annotation: Add comments and annotations to the assembly code to document important findings, observations, and hypotheses. This helps in creating a comprehensive analysis report and sharing insights with other analysts.

Remember, analyzing assembly code can be challenging, especially when dealing with complex or obfuscated malware. Continuously refer to reference materials, seek community support, and leverage specialized tools like disassemblers and debuggers to assist in code analysis. Over time, with practice and experience, analyzing assembly code becomes more efficient and effective in understanding malware behavior and developing appropriate countermeasures.

7.3 FUNCTION IDENTIFICATION

Identifying functions within the assembly code is a critical step in malware analysis. Functions represent distinct units of code that perform specific tasks or implement certain functionalities. By identifying and understanding these functions, analysts can gain insights into the malware's behavior and purpose. Here are some techniques for function identification in assembly code analysis:

1. Analyzing Function Prologues and Epilogues:

* Function prologue: Look for the instructions at the beginning of a function that set up the function's stack frame, such as pushing the base pointer (BP) and setting the stack pointer (SP).

* Function epilogue: Look for the instructions at the end of a function that clean up the stack and restore the original

state, such as restoring the base pointer and returning control to the calling function.

2. Recognizing Function Call Patterns:

   * Call instructions: Identify call instructions (e.g., CALL) that indicate a function call. Look for calls to external libraries or system functions (API calls) that suggest interaction with the operating system or other software components.

   * Function arguments: Observe how function arguments are passed, whether through registers, the stack, or a combination. Note any modifications or references to the arguments within the function.

   * Return values: Identify instructions that store the return value of a function, typically in registers like EAX or a designated memory location.

3. Control Flow Analysis:

   * Branch instructions: Identify conditional and unconditional branch instructions (e.g., JMP, JNZ, JZ) that control the flow of execution within the code. Follow the branches to locate code blocks that correspond to separate functions.

   * Function prologue analysis: Analyze the instructions before a branch or jump to determine if it signifies the start of a new function.

4. Data Flow Analysis:

   * Registers and memory access: Analyze the usage of registers and memory locations within the code. Look for instructions that read from or write to specific memory locations, which may indicate the start or end of a function.

   * Variable references: Observe instructions that modify or reference specific variables or data structures. These instructions may provide clues about the boundaries of a function.

5. Code Structure and Patterns:

   * Code repetition: Look for repetitive code patterns that indicate the presence of a function. Identifying similar

instruction sequences in different parts of the code may suggest the reuse of a function.

* Standard library functions: Recognize commonly used functions from standard libraries that exhibit well-known patterns or calling conventions.

6. Naming Conventions:

* Symbolic information: If available, use symbolic information like debug symbols or symbol tables to identify functions by their names. These names may provide insight into the purpose or functionality of the functions.

7. Collaborative Analysis:

* Community resources: Consult public resources, forums, or databases that provide information on known functions in specific malware families. These resources can help in quickly identifying commonly used functions.

It's important to note that identifying functions accurately can be challenging, especially in the presence of obfuscation techniques or complex control flow structures. Cross-referencing multiple analysis techniques, including static and dynamic analysis, can improve the accuracy of function identification. Additionally, documenting and organizing identified functions in a systematic manner enhances the overall understanding of the malware's structure and behavior.

7.4 MALWARE LOGIC AND FUNCTIONALITY

Understanding the logic and functionality of malware is a fundamental aspect of malware reverse engineering. By comprehending how the malware operates, analysts can identify its capabilities, intentions, and potential impact. Here are some key considerations for analyzing the logic and functionality of malware:

1. Behavioral Analysis:

* System interactions: Identify how the malware interacts with the underlying operating system, including file operations, network communication, registry modifications, and process/thread manipulation.

* Persistence mechanisms: Determine how the malware establishes persistence on the infected system, such as through startup entries, registry keys, scheduled tasks, or service installation.

* Self-defense mechanisms: Analyze any techniques employed by the malware to evade detection or hinder analysis, such as anti-debugging tricks, code obfuscation, or encryption.

* Information gathering: Identify if the malware collects sensitive information from the infected system, such as login credentials, financial data, or personally identifiable information.

2. Command and Control (C2) Communication:

* Network protocols: Determine the protocols used by the malware to communicate with its command and control infrastructure. Analyze the network traffic and payload structures to understand the communication mechanisms.

* Data exfiltration: Identify how the malware transfers stolen data or received commands to and from the command and control servers. This includes analyzing encryption, compression, or encoding techniques used for data concealment.

* Communication patterns: Observe the frequency, timing, and patterns of communication to detect any beaconing or command synchronization behaviors.

3. Payload Execution:

* Code injection: Identify any code injection techniques employed by the malware, such as process hollowing, DLL injection, or hooking, to execute its payload within legitimate processes.

* Malicious payload: Analyze the functionality of the payload executed by the malware, such as downloading and executing additional modules, launching denial-of-service attacks, or propagating to other systems.

4. Malware Families and Variants:

   *   Malware classification: Determine if the analyzed malware belongs to any known malware families or if it exhibits characteristics of a specific type, such as ransomware, trojan, botnet, or rootkit.

   *   Variant analysis: Compare the analyzed malware with known variants or samples to identify similarities or differences in behavior and functionality.

5. Code Reuse and Dependencies:

   *   External libraries and APIs: Identify any external libraries or APIs used by the malware for specific functionalities. Understanding the functions and capabilities provided by these libraries can shed light on the malware's intended operations.

   *   Code reuse: Analyze if the malware reuses code snippets or techniques from previously known malware or open-source projects. This can provide insights into the author's skills, motivations, or affiliations.

6. Malware Evolution:

   *   Versioning and updates: Determine if the analyzed malware has different versions or if it receives updates over time. Analyze the differences between versions to understand enhancements, changes in behavior, or new features.

   *   Malware campaigns: Investigate if the analyzed malware is part of a larger campaign or if it shares similarities with other reported incidents. This can provide context and help in attributing the malware to specific threat actors or groups.

7. Documentation and Reporting:

   *   Detailed analysis: Document the observed behavior, functionality, and identified capabilities of the malware. Include information on relevant artifacts, system changes, or indicators of compromise (IOCs).

* Indirect effects: Consider the potential impact of the malware beyond its immediate functionality. This includes its ability to propagate, launch secondary attacks, or compromise other systems or devices.

Analyzing the logic and functionality of malware requires a combination of static and dynamic analysis techniques, as well as knowledge of malware behavior patterns and common techniques used by threat actors. Continuously updating and sharing analysis findings with the broader security community helps in building a collective understanding of emerging threats and effective countermeasures.

Chapter 8

MALWARE BEHAVIOR ANALYSIS

Malware behavior analysis is a crucial aspect of understanding the actions and intentions of malicious software. By analyzing the behavior of malware, analysts can gain insights into its capabilities, potential impact, and the risks it poses. Here are key considerations for conducting malware behavior analysis:

1. Initial Analysis:

   * Execution environment: Analyze the malware's behavior in a controlled and isolated environment to observe its initial actions upon execution. Monitor changes to the system, such as new processes, file modifications, registry modifications, or network connections.

   * Process and thread behavior: Study how the malware creates, terminates, or manipulates processes and threads within the infected system. Identify any suspicious or abnormal process behavior.

2. System Interactions:

   * File operations: Monitor file creation, modification, and deletion activities performed by the malware. Identify which files are targeted and understand their purpose within the malware's functionality.

   * Registry modifications: Analyze changes to the system registry made by the malware. Look for modifications to startup entries, security settings, or other critical registry keys.

✻   Network communication: Capture and analyze network traffic generated by the malware. Identify communication protocols, destination IP addresses, and the type of data being transmitted. This helps in understanding the malware's command and control (C2) communication, data exfiltration, or potential propagation methods.

✻   Process injection and manipulation: Observe if the malware injects code into legitimate processes or manipulates their behavior. This technique is often used to evade detection and carry out malicious activities within trusted processes.

3. Malware Persistence:

✻   Startup mechanisms: Identify how the malware establishes persistence on the infected system, such as through modifications to startup entries, scheduled tasks, or service installations.

✻   Hooking and code injection: Analyze techniques used by the malware to maintain persistence, such as hooking system functions or injecting code into critical system processes.

✻   Rootkit capabilities: Detect if the malware possesses rootkit functionalities that enable it to hide its presence, processes, files, or network connections from security mechanisms.

4. Data Manipulation and Theft:

✻   Data exfiltration: Determine if the malware steals sensitive information from the infected system. Analyze the methods used for data exfiltration, such as network protocols, encryption, or covert channels.

✻   Keylogging and screen capturing: Identify if the malware logs keystrokes or captures screenshots to collect sensitive information, such as login credentials or financial data.

✻   Cryptocurrency mining: Analyze if the malware utilizes system resources for cryptocurrency mining, leading to increased CPU or GPU usage.

5. Malware Payloads and Capabilities:

✻   Additional module download: Determine if the malware downloads and executes additional modules or payloads from external sources. Analyze the purpose and functionality of these modules.

* Exploitation of vulnerabilities: Identify if the malware exploits software vulnerabilities to gain unauthorized access, propagate to other systems, or escalate privileges.

* Botnet functionality: Investigate if the malware is part of a botnet, capable of receiving commands from a command and control server, participating in distributed denial-of-service (DDoS) attacks, or engaging in other coordinated activities.

6. Analysis Automation and Sandboxing:

* Automated analysis: Leverage automated analysis tools and sandboxes to analyze the behavior of malware samples in a controlled environment. These tools provide insights into the actions performed by the malware and help identify patterns or signatures associated with malicious behavior.

* Behavioral indicators: Identify and document behavioral indicators of malware, such as specific file or registry modifications, network traffic patterns, or process behavior. These indicators can assist in developing detection and mitigation strategies.

7. Collaboration and Threat Intelligence:

* Information sharing: Collaborate with other analysts and share insights, indicators, and behavioral patterns with the broader security community. This facilitates the collective understanding of malware behavior and helps in developing proactive defenses.

* Threat intelligence: Utilize threat intelligence feeds and databases to gather information on known malware behaviors, patterns, and indicators. Stay updated with emerging threats and incorporate this knowledge into behavioral analysis.

Malware behavior analysis requires a combination of manual analysis techniques, automated tools, and continuous learning from the ever-evolving threat landscape. By understanding the behavior and intentions of malware, analysts can develop effective detection, mitigation, and response strategies to protect systems and networks from malicious activities.

8.1 MALWARE CLASSIFICATION

Malware classification is the process of categorizing malicious software based on its characteristics, behavior, and intended purpose. Classifying malware helps in understanding its nature, identifying common traits among different samples, and developing effective countermeasures. Here are some common categories of malware:

1. Viruses:

    * Viruses are self-replicating programs that attach themselves to legitimate files or programs and spread by infecting other files or systems. They can cause damage to files, disrupt system functionality, or enable unauthorized access.

2. Worms:

    * Worms are standalone programs that can self-replicate and spread across networks or systems without requiring a host file. They often exploit security vulnerabilities to propagate and can cause widespread damage by consuming network resources or launching other malicious activities.

3. Trojans:

    * Trojans disguise themselves as legitimate software or files to deceive users. Once executed, they perform malicious actions, such as stealing sensitive information, modifying system settings, or providing unauthorized access to the attacker.

4. Ransomware:

    * Ransomware encrypts files on the victim's system and demands a ransom payment in exchange for the decryption key. It is designed to extort money from individuals or organizations by denying access to their own data.

5. Spyware:

    * Spyware is designed to monitor user activities, gather sensitive information, and transmit it to a remote server

without the user's consent. It can capture keystrokes, track browsing habits, collect personal data, or record audio/video.

6. Adware:

   * Adware displays unwanted advertisements, often in the form of pop-ups or browser redirects, to generate revenue for the attacker. It may collect user information to target advertisements or compromise the user's browsing experience.

7. Botnets:

   * Botnets consist of a network of compromised computers (bots) controlled by a central command and control (C2) server. Botnets are used for various malicious activities, including distributed denial-of-service (DDoS) attacks, spam distribution, or cryptocurrency mining.

8. Rootkits:

   * Rootkits are designed to conceal malicious activities and maintain unauthorized access to a compromised system. They modify system components or kernel-level code to hide their presence from security tools and evade detection.

9. Backdoors:

   * Backdoors provide unauthorized access to a compromised system, bypassing normal authentication mechanisms. They allow attackers to maintain persistence, execute commands, or control the compromised system remotely.

10. Keyloggers:

   * Keyloggers record keystrokes entered by users and capture sensitive information such as passwords, credit card details, or other confidential data. The captured information is often transmitted to the attacker.

These categories are not mutually exclusive, and many malware samples exhibit characteristics of multiple types. Additionally, malware can evolve over time, incorporating new features and techniques to evade detection.

Malware classification is an ongoing process as new malware variants emerge and existing ones evolve. Analysts and security researchers continuously study and analyze malware samples to identify patterns, behaviors, and relationships between different samples. This knowledge is shared through collaborative efforts, such as threat intelligence sharing platforms, to enhance the collective ability to detect, mitigate, and respond to malware threats effectively.

8.2 MALWARE FUNCTIONALITY IDENTIFICATION

Identifying the functionality of malware is a critical aspect of malware analysis. Understanding how malware operates and the specific actions it performs enables analysts to assess the potential impact, determine the appropriate mitigation strategies, and develop effective countermeasures. Here are key considerations for identifying the functionality of malware:

1. Code Analysis:

    * Disassembly: Disassemble the malware's executable file to obtain the low-level assembly code. Analyze the code to identify the functions, routines, and algorithms used by the malware.

    * Decompilation: Convert the malware's binary code into a higher-level programming language representation to gain insights into its logic and functionality.

2. Behavioral Analysis:

    * Dynamic analysis: Execute the malware in a controlled environment or sandbox to observe its behavior. Monitor system interactions, file operations, registry modifications, network communications, and any other actions performed by the malware.

    * System monitoring: Use system monitoring tools to capture and analyze the malware's activities, such as process creation, file system changes, network traffic, and API calls. This helps identify the specific functionality and actions of the malware.

3. Function Identification:

   * Function calls: Identify the functions or APIs (Application Programming Interfaces) called by the malware. Analyze these function calls to understand the actions performed, such as file manipulation, network communication, registry modifications, or process manipulation.

   * Cryptographic operations: Look for cryptographic function calls used by the malware, such as encryption, decryption, or hashing. This indicates potential data manipulation, communication security, or obfuscation techniques used by the malware.

   * Code patterns: Analyze code patterns and algorithms used by the malware to identify specific functionalities, such as keylogging, remote access, data exfiltration, or payload execution.

4. Payload Execution:

   * Additional module download: Determine if the malware downloads and executes additional modules or payloads from external sources. Analyze the purpose and functionality of these modules.

   * Exploitation of vulnerabilities: Identify if the malware exploits software vulnerabilities to gain unauthorized access, propagate to other systems, or escalate privileges.

   * Malicious activities: Observe the actions performed by the malware, such as launching denial-of-service attacks, participating in botnet activities, mining cryptocurrency, or carrying out data theft.

5. Command and Control (C2) Communication:

   * Network traffic analysis: Monitor and analyze network communications initiated by the malware. Identify the protocols, destinations, and data exchanged to understand the communication mechanisms and potential commands received from the command and control server.

   * Data exfiltration: Determine if the malware steals sensitive information from the infected system and transmits it

to remote servers. Analyze the methods used for data exfiltration, such as encryption, encoding, or covert channels.

6. Anti-analysis and Evasion Techniques:

   * Obfuscation: Look for code obfuscation techniques used by the malware to evade detection, such as code encryption, packing, or use of polymorphic code.

   * Anti-debugging techniques: Identify if the malware employs anti-debugging mechanisms to hinder analysis, such as checking for debuggers, injecting code into legitimate processes, or modifying code during runtime.

7. Documentation and Reporting:

   * Detailed analysis: Document the observed behavior, identified functionality, and potential impact of the malware. Include information on relevant artifacts, system changes, or indicators of compromise (IOCs).

   * Indirect effects: Consider the potential secondary effects of the malware beyond its immediate functionality, such as propagation methods, secondary payloads, or lateral movement techniques.

Malware functionality identification requires a combination of static and dynamic analysis techniques, as well as expertise in reverse engineering, programming languages, and malware behavior patterns. Continuous learning, collaboration with the security community, and staying updated with emerging malware trends are crucial for accurate functionality identification and effective mitigation strategies.

8.3 MALICIOUS ACTIVITIES ANALYSIS

Analyzing the malicious activities performed by malware is a crucial step in understanding its impact, assessing the level of risk, and developing appropriate mitigation strategies. By identifying the specific actions carried out by malware, analysts can gain insights into its intentions, potential targets, and potential damage it can cause. Here are key considerations for analyzing malicious activities:

1. Data Theft and Exfiltration:

   * Data collection: Determine if the malware is designed to steal sensitive information from the infected system, such as login credentials, financial data, or personal information.

   * Data exfiltration methods: Identify the techniques employed by the malware to transmit stolen data to remote servers or command and control (C2) infrastructure. This may include encryption, encoding, or using covert channels to bypass detection.

2. Remote Access and Control:

   * Backdoor functionality: Determine if the malware provides unauthorized access to the compromised system, allowing remote attackers to control and manipulate the infected system.

   * Command and control (C2) communication: Analyze the communication channels and protocols used by the malware to receive commands and instructions from a remote server. This helps understand the level of control the malware provides to the attacker.

3. Payload Execution:

   * Secondary payload delivery: Identify if the malware is capable of downloading and executing additional payloads or modules from external sources. Analyze the purpose and functionality of these payloads.

   * Exploitation of vulnerabilities: Determine if the malware exploits software vulnerabilities to gain unauthorized access, propagate to other systems, or escalate privileges.

4. Botnet Activities:

   * Botnet participation: Investigate if the malware is part of a larger botnet network, contributing to coordinated activities such as distributed denial-of-service (DDoS) attacks, spam distribution, or cryptocurrency mining.

   * Command propagation: Analyze how the malware receives and executes commands from the botnet controller, as well as the specific activities it carries out on behalf of the botnet.

5. System Disruption and Damage:

   * File system modifications: Identify if the malware modifies or deletes critical system files, disrupts file integrity, or encrypts files to cause damage or denial of access.

   * System performance degradation: Determine if the malware consumes excessive system resources, leading to reduced performance, system crashes, or instability.

   * System configuration changes: Analyze if the malware modifies system settings, security configurations, or network parameters to compromise the system's integrity or disrupt normal operation.

6. Propagation and Lateral Movement:

   * Worm-like behavior: Identify if the malware exhibits self-replicating capabilities, spreading across networks or systems without direct user interaction.

   * Exploitation of network vulnerabilities: Determine if the malware exploits network vulnerabilities to gain unauthorized access to other systems within the network, establishing a foothold for further attacks.

7. Impact on Privacy and User Experience:

   * Privacy violations: Analyze if the malware invades user privacy by capturing sensitive information, monitoring user activities, or intercepting communication channels.

   * User experience degradation: Identify if the malware disrupts the user experience by displaying unwanted advertisements, redirecting web traffic, or modifying browser settings.

8. Persistence Mechanisms:

   * Startup mechanisms: Determine how the malware establishes persistence on the infected system, such as modifying startup entries, creating scheduled tasks, or installing services.

   * Anti-analysis and evasion techniques: Identify if the malware employs techniques to evade detection, such as

anti-debugging mechanisms, code obfuscation, or anti-forensic capabilities.

9. Reporting and Documentation:

   * Detailed analysis: Document the observed malicious activities, potential targets, and impact of the malware. Include information on relevant indicators of compromise (IOCs), network traffic patterns, and system changes.

   * - Indirect effects: Consider the potential secondary effects of the malware beyond its immediate activities, such as lateral movement, propagation methods, or collateral damage to other systems or networks.

Analyzing malicious activities requires a combination of static and dynamic analysis techniques, as well as expertise in reverse engineering, network analysis, and malware behavior patterns. It is essential to stay updated with the latest malware trends, collaborate with the security community, and leverage threat intelligence sources to enhance the accuracy and effectiveness of malicious activities analysis.

8.4 CODE TRACING AND EXECUTION FLOW

Code tracing and understanding the execution flow of malware is a critical aspect of malware analysis. It helps analysts gain insights into how the malware operates, the sequence of actions it performs, and the potential impact on the infected system. Here are key considerations for code tracing and execution flow analysis:

1. Dynamic Analysis:

   * Debugging: Use a debugger to trace the execution flow of the malware in a controlled environment. Set breakpoints, step through the code, and examine the values of variables and registers at different points in the execution.

   * Dynamic analysis tools: Utilize dynamic analysis tools that capture the runtime behavior of the malware, such as process monitors or system monitoring tools. These tools provide insights into system calls, API invocations, and file/registry operations performed by the malware.

2. Function Calls:

   ✳ API Monitoring: Identify the Application Programming Interfaces (APIs) called by the malware. Monitor API calls to understand the interactions with the operating system, file system, network, and other system components.

   ✳ Function-level analysis: Analyze the functions or subroutines within the malware code. Identify the purpose and functionality of each function to comprehend the overall behavior of the malware.

3. Control Flow Analysis:

   ✳ Branch instructions: Analyze branch instructions (e.g., conditional jumps, loops, function calls) to understand the different paths the malware can take during execution. Trace the flow of execution through these branches to determine the conditions that influence the malware's behavior.

   ✳ Control flow graphs: Construct control flow graphs to visualize the flow of execution within the malware. This helps identify the relationships between different functions, loops, and conditional statements.

4. Dynamic Memory Analysis:

   ✳ Heap and stack analysis: Monitor and analyze the malware's interaction with dynamically allocated memory. Track memory allocations, deallocations, and modifications to understand how the malware manages and utilizes memory resources during execution.

   ✳ Memory content examination: Inspect the content of memory locations accessed by the malware to uncover important data structures, encryption keys, or other runtime artifacts that may reveal the malware's functionality.

5. Code Reconstruction:

   ✳ Disassembly and decompilation: Disassemble the malware's binary code to obtain the low-level assembly instructions. Decompile the code to obtain a higher-level representation, such as C or C++, to facilitate code analysis and understanding.

   ✳ Control flow reconstruction: Reconstruct the control flow of the malware by analyzing the disassembled code and identifying the relationships between different code blocks, functions, and loops.

6. Documentation and Reporting:

   ✳ Detailed analysis: Document the findings from code tracing and execution flow analysis. Describe the sequence of actions performed by the malware, important functions or routines, and the overall execution flow.

   ✳ Indicators of compromise (IOCs): Identify any unique code patterns, function names, or specific instructions that can be used as IOCs to detect the presence of similar malware.

Code tracing and execution flow analysis require a deep understanding of assembly language, programming concepts, and debugging techniques. It is important to combine static and dynamic analysis approaches to gain a comprehensive understanding of the malware's behavior. Continuous learning, hands-on experience, and collaboration with the security community are crucial for effective code tracing and execution flow analysis.

Chapter 9

MALWARE DETECTION AND MITIGATION

Detecting and mitigating malware is a crucial aspect of cybersecurity. It involves implementing strategies and measures to identify, prevent, and respond to malicious software threats. Here are key considerations for malware detection and mitigation:

1. Antivirus and Anti-Malware Solutions:

    *   Implement reputable antivirus and anti-malware software on all systems. Regularly update the software and virus definitions to ensure protection against the latest threats.

    *   Enable real-time scanning to detect and block malware as it is encountered.

    *   Schedule regular system scans to identify and remove any existing malware infections.

2. Network Security:

    *   Deploy network security solutions, such as firewalls, intrusion detection systems (IDS), and intrusion prevention systems (IPS), to monitor and filter incoming and outgoing network traffic.

    *   Utilize network behavior analysis tools to detect anomalous activities indicative of malware infections or malicious network behavior.

3. Email Security:

    *   Implement robust email security measures, including spam filters, email attachment scanning, and anti-phishing mechanisms.

❋ Educate users about safe email practices, such as avoiding opening suspicious email attachments or clicking on links from unknown or untrusted sources.

4. User Education and Awareness:

    ❋ Conduct regular security awareness training to educate users about common malware threats, social engineering techniques, and safe browsing habits.

    ❋ Encourage users to exercise caution when downloading files, visiting websites, or clicking on links, especially from unknown or untrusted sources.

5. Patch Management:

    ❋ Keep operating systems, applications, and software up to date by regularly applying security patches and updates. This helps address vulnerabilities that malware may exploit.

6. Secure Web Browsing:

    ❋ Implement web filtering and content filtering solutions to block access to malicious websites, known malware distribution sites, and suspicious web content.

    ❋ Enforce secure browsing practices, such as using HTTPS for website communication and avoiding visiting untrusted or potentially malicious websites.

7. Behavioral Analysis and Anomaly Detection:

    ❋ Implement advanced threat detection solutions that use behavioral analysis and machine learning algorithms to identify patterns and anomalies indicative of malware activity.

    ❋ Monitor system and network behavior for unusual activities, such as unauthorized access attempts, suspicious file modifications, or abnormal network traffic.

8. Incident Response:

    ❋ Develop an incident response plan that outlines the steps to be taken in the event of a malware infection. This includes isolating affected systems, collecting evidence, and conducting forensic analysis.

* Establish communication channels and reporting procedures to ensure swift response and coordination among stakeholders.

9. Backup and Recovery:

* Regularly back up critical data and systems to ensure the ability to restore operations in the event of a malware attack.

* Test the backup and recovery procedures periodically to verify their effectiveness.

10. Security Information and Event Management (SIEM):

* Implement a SIEM solution to centralize and analyze security events and logs from various systems. This helps detect and respond to potential malware incidents more effectively.

11. Threat Intelligence:

* Stay updated with the latest malware trends, indicators of compromise (IOCs), and emerging threats by leveraging threat intelligence feeds, security advisories, and information sharing platforms.

* Collaborate with industry peers and security communities to exchange information and gain insights into new malware variants and attack techniques.

12. Continuous Monitoring and Improvement:

* Regularly review and update security measures to adapt to evolving malware threats and emerging technologies.

* Conduct periodic security assessments, penetration testing, and vulnerability scanning to identify and address potential weaknesses in the security infrastructure.

By implementing a multi-layered defense approach, staying proactive with security measures, and fostering a culture of security awareness, organizations can effectively detect and mitigate malware threats, minimizing the potential impact on their systems and data.

9.1 SIGNATURE-BASED DETECTION

Signature-based detection is one of the traditional and widely used methods for identifying and detecting known malware. It involves comparing files or code snippets against a database of pre-defined signatures or patterns associated with known malware. Here are key considerations for signature-based detection:

1. Signature Generation:

   * Malware samples: Security researchers analyze malware samples and extract unique characteristics, such as specific strings, byte sequences, or code snippets that are indicative of the malware's presence.

   * Signature creation: Based on the extracted characteristics, signatures or patterns are generated. These signatures can be in the form of hash values, regular expressions, or specific byte sequences.

2. Signature Database:

   * Signature repository: Maintain a database or signature repository that contains the signatures of known malware. This database is regularly updated as new malware samples are discovered and analyzed.

   * Vendor updates: Ensure that antivirus or anti-malware software is configured to receive regular updates from the vendor's signature database. These updates include the latest signatures for detecting newly discovered malware.

3. Scanning and Detection:

   * File scanning: When a file is accessed or executed, it is compared against the signatures in the database. If a match is found, the file is flagged as potentially malicious.

   * On-demand scanning: Perform scheduled or manual scans of files, directories, or entire systems to identify malware based on matching signatures.

   * Real-time scanning: Enable real-time or on-access scanning, which continuously monitors files and processes as they are accessed or executed.

4. Limitations of Signature-based Detection:

*   New or unknown malware: Signature-based detection is effective only against known malware. It may not detect new or previously unseen malware for which signatures have not been created yet.

*   Signature updates: The effectiveness of signature-based detection relies on timely updates to the signature database. Delayed updates may result in the inability to detect newly emerging malware.

*   Polymorphic and encrypted malware: Malware that employs techniques like code obfuscation, polymorphism, or encryption can evade signature-based detection by altering their signatures or behavior.

*   Targeted attacks: Sophisticated malware designed for targeted attacks may not have widely known signatures, making them difficult to detect using signature-based methods.

5. Supplementing with Other Techniques:

*   Heuristics and behavior-based analysis: Combine signature-based detection with heuristics and behavior-based analysis to detect unknown or zero-day malware that may not have signatures available.

*   Sandbox analysis: Employ sandboxing techniques to execute suspicious files or code in an isolated environment and observe their behavior. This helps detect malware that exhibits malicious activities but may not have known signatures.

*   Machine learning and AI-based approaches: Utilize machine learning and artificial intelligence techniques to analyze large volumes of data, identify patterns, and detect previously unseen malware based on behavioral characteristics.

Signature-based detection remains an important component of a comprehensive malware detection strategy. While it has limitations in detecting new and sophisticated malware, it is effective in identifying known malware and providing an initial layer of defense. Integrating multiple detection techniques, staying up to date with signature updates, and leveraging advanced detection mechanisms enhance the overall effectiveness of malware detection and mitigation efforts.

9.2 BEHAVIOR-BASED DETECTION

Behavior-based detection is an approach to malware detection that focuses on analyzing the behavior and activities of software to identify malicious or suspicious actions. Instead of relying on pre-defined signatures, behavior-based detection monitors the runtime behavior of applications, processes, or systems to identify abnormal or malicious activities. Here are key considerations for behavior-based detection:

1. Baseline Behavior:

   * Establish a baseline of normal behavior for systems, processes, or applications. This baseline represents the expected and legitimate activities.

   * Monitor and analyze system activities, network communications, file operations, and process behaviors to understand the typical behavior of a clean and properly functioning system.

2. Anomaly Detection:

   * Identify deviations from the established baseline behavior. This involves detecting activities that significantly differ from what is considered normal or expected.

   * Employ statistical analysis, machine learning algorithms, or rule-based systems to identify anomalies based on variations in resource usage, network traffic patterns, or system interactions.

3. Indicators of Compromise (IOCs):

   * Define and monitor indicators of compromise (IOCs) that indicate potentially malicious behavior. These can include specific patterns of system calls, API invocations, network connections, or file operations associated with known malware or attack techniques.

- ✳ Continuously update and expand the list of IOCs based on emerging threats and security intelligence sources.

4. Dynamic Analysis:

- ✳ Execute suspicious files or code samples in a controlled environment, such as a sandbox, to observe their behavior and interactions with the system.

- ✳ Monitor and log system activities, network traffic, file modifications, and process behaviors during the execution. Analyze these logs to identify any malicious or suspicious actions.

5. Network Traffic Analysis:

- ✳ Monitor and analyze network traffic for indicators of malicious behavior, such as communication with known command and control (C2) servers, data exfiltration, or unusual network protocols.

- ✳ Employ network intrusion detection systems (NIDS) or deep packet inspection (DPI) tools to identify abnormal network patterns or anomalies indicative of malware activity.

6. System Monitoring:

- ✳ Utilize system monitoring tools, such as host-based intrusion detection systems (HIDS) or endpoint detection and response (EDR) solutions, to capture and analyze system activities, including process creations, file modifications, registry changes, and network connections.

- ✳ Analyze the collected data to detect patterns or behaviors that deviate from normal system operation.

7. Machine Learning and AI:

- ✳ Apply machine learning algorithms or artificial intelligence techniques to analyze large datasets and identify patterns associated with malicious behavior.

- ✳ Train models using labeled datasets of known good and malicious behavior to develop predictive models that can detect and classify unknown or previously unseen malware based on their behavior.

8. Continuous Monitoring and Analysis:

    *   Implement real-time or near real-time monitoring of system and network activities to promptly detect and respond to potential malware incidents.

    *   Continuously analyze collected data, identify new behavioral patterns, and update detection rules or models accordingly.

9. Collaboration and Threat Intelligence:

    *   Participate in information sharing initiatives and collaborate with the security community to gain insights into emerging threats, attack techniques, and behavioral indicators.

    *   Leverage threat intelligence feeds and security advisories to stay updated with the latest information on known malware behaviors and indicators of compromise.

Behavior-based detection provides a proactive approach to identifying and mitigating malware by focusing on the actions and behaviors exhibited by software. By monitoring and analyzing runtime behaviors, organizations can detect previously unseen or unknown malware, including zero-day threats. Integrating behavior-based detection with other detection techniques, such as signature-based detection and sandbox analysis, enhances the overall effectiveness of malware detection and strengthens the security posture of systems and networks.

9.3 MACHINE LEARNING IN MALWARE DETECTION

Machine learning has emerged as a powerful tool in malware detection due to its ability to analyze large datasets, identify patterns, and make predictions based on learned models. By leveraging machine learning algorithms, malware detection systems can effectively identify and classify both known and unknown malware samples. Here are key considerations for using machine learning in malware detection:

1. Feature Extraction:
   - Determine relevant features that can represent the characteristics of malware samples. These features can include static attributes such as file size, file type, or code structure, as well as dynamic behaviors such as system calls, network traffic patterns, or API invocations.
   - Extract features from the malware samples using techniques like static analysis, dynamic analysis, or disassembly.
2. Dataset Preparation:
   - Collect and curate a labeled dataset consisting of both malware samples and benign files. The dataset should represent a diverse range of malware families and benign software.
   - Ensure the dataset is well-balanced and contains sufficient samples for each class to avoid bias during training.
3. Training and Model Development:
   - Select appropriate machine learning algorithms based on the nature of the data and the desired detection objectives. Commonly used algorithms include decision trees, random forests, support vector machines (SVM), and deep learning models like convolutional neural networks (CNN) or recurrent neural networks (RNN).
   - Divide the dataset into training and testing sets. Use the training set to train the machine learning model on the extracted features and associated labels.
   - Optimize the model by tuning hyperparameters, such as learning rate, regularization parameters, or architecture configuration, using techniques like cross-validation or grid search.
4. Feature Selection and Dimensionality Reduction:
   - Apply feature selection techniques to identify the most relevant and informative features for malware detection. This helps improve the efficiency and accuracy of the model by reducing noise and focusing on the most discriminative attributes.

✳ Use dimensionality reduction techniques, such as principal component analysis (PCA) or t-distributed stochastic neighbor embedding (t-SNE), to reduce the dimensionality of the feature space and visualize the data.

5. Model Evaluation and Validation:

   ✳ Evaluate the trained model using the testing set to assess its performance metrics, such as accuracy, precision, recall, or F1 score.

   ✳ Conduct cross-validation or use separate validation datasets to validate the model's generalization ability and assess its performance on unseen data.

   ✳ Continuously refine and update the model based on feedback, new samples, or evolving malware characteristics.

6. Ensemble Techniques and Transfer Learning:

   ✳ Explore ensemble techniques, such as bagging, boosting, or stacking, to combine multiple machine learning models for improved detection performance.

   ✳ Consider transfer learning approaches, where models pre-trained on large datasets can be fine-tuned or used as feature extractors for malware detection tasks.

7. Real-time Detection and Deployment:

   ✳ Implement the trained machine learning model into a real-time malware detection system. This can involve integrating it with existing security infrastructure or deploying it as a standalone solution.

   ✳ Ensure the detection system can handle large volumes of incoming data with low latency to provide timely and efficient detection capabilities.

   ✳ Monitor the performance of the detection system in production and update the model periodically to adapt to evolving malware threats.

8. Adversarial Robustness:

   ✳ Consider adversarial attacks where attackers attempt to manipulate or evade machine learning-based detection systems. Apply techniques like adversarial training, input sanitization, or anomaly detection to enhance the robustness of the model against adversarial samples.

Machine learning in malware detection enables automated and scalable analysis of malware samples, allowing for the identification of both known and unknown threats. It enhances the efficiency and accuracy of malware detection systems, providing organizations with proactive defense capabilities against evolving and sophisticated malware attacks. Continuous research, collaboration, and integration of machine learning techniques into security frameworks are essential to stay ahead of emerging malware threats.

9.4 INCIDENT RESPONSE AND MITIGATION STRATEGIES

Incident response and mitigation strategies are crucial for effectively handling and containing malware incidents within an organization. These strategies involve a systematic approach to identify, respond to, and recover from security incidents involving malware. Here are key considerations for incident response and mitigation:

1. Incident Response Plan:

   * Develop a comprehensive incident response plan that outlines the roles, responsibilities, and procedures to be followed in the event of a malware incident. This plan should include clear escalation paths, communication channels, and defined actions for different types of incidents.

2. Incident Identification and Triage:

   * Establish robust monitoring systems and network security controls to detect potential malware incidents in real-time. Monitor system logs, network traffic, and security alerts to identify signs of compromise or malicious activity.

   * Conduct rapid triage to determine the severity and impact of the incident. Assess the affected systems, network assets, and data to prioritize response efforts.

3. Containment and Isolation:

   * Isolate the affected systems or devices from the network to prevent further spread of malware. Disconnect

compromised systems from the network to minimize potential damage or unauthorized access.

- Preserve evidence by taking snapshots of affected systems or collecting relevant log files to aid in the investigation and subsequent analysis.

4. Malware Analysis:

- Conduct a thorough analysis of the malware to understand its behavior, functionality, and potential impact. Use static and dynamic analysis techniques, sandboxing, or specialized malware analysis tools to gain insights into the malware's characteristics.

- Determine the malware's persistence mechanisms, communication channels, and any potential secondary payloads or actions it may perform.

5. Eradication and Remediation:

- Develop a remediation plan to remove the malware from the affected systems. This may involve utilizing antivirus software, applying security patches, removing malicious files, or restoring systems from clean backups.

- Identify and address any vulnerabilities or weaknesses that contributed to the malware incident, such as outdated software, misconfigurations, or insecure user practices.

6. Communication and Reporting:

- Establish clear communication channels to notify relevant stakeholders, including IT teams, management, legal personnel, and affected users.

- Prepare incident reports detailing the nature of the incident, the actions taken, and recommendations to prevent similar incidents in the future.

- Comply with any legal or regulatory requirements regarding incident reporting and disclosure.

7. System Recovery and Restoration:

- Restore affected systems from clean backups or rebuild compromised systems using trusted installation media and verified software sources.

✽ Validate the integrity and security of restored systems before reintegrating them into the network.

8. Lessons Learned and Continuous Improvement:

✽ Conduct post-incident reviews to identify lessons learned and areas for improvement in incident response procedures, security controls, and employee awareness and training.

✽ Update incident response plans based on the insights gained from the incident to enhance future incident handling capabilities.

9. Proactive Security Measures:

✽ Implement proactive security measures, such as regular vulnerability assessments, penetration testing, security awareness training, and access controls, to reduce the risk of future malware incidents.

✽ Stay updated with the latest security patches, threat intelligence feeds, and emerging malware trends to proactively identify and address potential vulnerabilities.

10. Collaboration and External Support:

✽ Collaborate with internal teams, external incident response service providers, or cybersecurity organizations to obtain expert assistance and guidance during incident response and mitigation efforts.

✽ Engage with relevant law enforcement agencies, if necessary, to report the incident and cooperate in the investigation.

Effective incident response and mitigation strategies help organizations minimize the impact of malware incidents, reduce recovery time, and strengthen overall security posture. By adopting a proactive and well-defined incident response plan, organizations can swiftly detect, contain, and recover from malware incidents while continuously improving their security practices.

Chapter 10
CASE STUDIES

Some examples of notable malware incidents from the past to illustrate the importance of malware analysis and the impact it can have. Here are a few case studies:

1. WannaCry Ransomware:

    The WannaCry ransomware attack occurred in May 2017 and targeted thousands of systems worldwide. It exploited a vulnerability in the Windows operating system to spread rapidly across networks. WannaCry encrypted files on infected systems and demanded ransom payments in Bitcoin for their release. The incident affected organizations across various sectors, including healthcare, finance, and government agencies. The analysis of the malware helped identify its propagation methods, encryption algorithms, and potential mitigations, leading to the development of security patches and detection signatures.

2. Stuxnet Worm:

    The Stuxnet worm, discovered in 2010, was a sophisticated malware designed to target and disrupt Iran's nuclear program. It specifically targeted industrial control systems (ICS) and exploited zero-day vulnerabilities to gain access and manipulate programmable logic controllers (PLCs) used in centrifuge operations. Stuxnet was a groundbreaking example of state-sponsored cyber warfare and highlighted the potential risks posed by advanced malware. Analyzing Stuxnet played a crucial role in understanding its unique characteristics, the vulnerabilities it targeted, and the potential implications for critical infrastructure security.

3. NotPetya Ransomware:

 The NotPetya ransomware attack occurred in June 2017 and caused widespread damage globally. It initially masqueraded as the Petya ransomware but was later identified as a destructive malware that aimed to disrupt systems rather than extort payments. NotPetya leveraged the EternalBlue exploit, similar to WannaCry, to spread across networks. It targeted organizations in various sectors, including shipping, manufacturing, and energy. Analyzing NotPetya helped uncover its destructive nature, propagation techniques, and the importance of patching vulnerable systems.

4. SolarWinds Supply Chain Attack:

 The SolarWinds supply chain attack, discovered in December 2020, was a highly sophisticated cyberattack that targeted organizations using the SolarWinds Orion IT management software. The attackers compromised the software build process, inserting a malicious backdoor into legitimate software updates. This allowed them to gain unauthorized access to the networks of numerous organizations, including government agencies and technology firms. Analyzing the malware involved in the SolarWinds attack was crucial in understanding its sophisticated techniques, lateral movement capabilities, and the need for enhanced supply chain security practices.

 These case studies highlight the significance of malware analysis in understanding the nature of threats, identifying their propagation methods, and developing effective mitigation strategies. Analyzing malware incidents provides valuable insights into attacker techniques, vulnerabilities, and potential countermeasures. By studying these incidents, security professionals can continuously improve their defenses and respond more effectively to emerging malware threats.

10.1 ANALYZING RANSOMWARE

Ransomware attacks have become increasingly prevalent and devastating in recent years. Analyzing ransomware is crucial for understanding its behavior, identifying its propagation methods, and developing effective mitigation strategies. Here are key aspects to consider when analyzing ransomware:

1. Sample Acquisition:

   * Obtain a sample of the ransomware for analysis. This can be done through controlled environments, honeypots, or collaboration with cybersecurity organizations.

   * Ensure proper precautions are taken to handle the ransomware sample securely and prevent unintended infections or data loss.

2. Static Analysis:

   * Conduct static analysis by examining the ransomware's code, structure, and other attributes without executing it.

   * Disassemble the code to understand its logic and functionality.

   * Identify any encryption algorithms, communication channels, or command and control (C2) infrastructure utilized by the ransomware.

3. Dynamic Analysis:

   * Execute the ransomware sample in a controlled environment, such as a virtual machine or sandbox, to observe its behavior.

   * Monitor system activities, file modifications, network traffic, and registry changes during execution.

   * Document and analyze the observed behaviors, including file encryption techniques, network communication protocols, and persistence mechanisms.

4. Network Traffic Analysis:

   Analyze network traffic generated by the ransomware to identify communication patterns and potential C2 infrastructure.

   Use network analysis tools to capture and inspect network packets for any indicators of compromise (IOCs) or malicious behavior.

Determine the encryption used for communication and extract any relevant encryption keys or configuration data.

5. Encryption Analysis:

   ❋ Analyze the ransomware's encryption methods to understand the strength and implementation details.

   ❋ Identify the encryption algorithms, key generation techniques, and key storage mechanisms used by the ransomware.

   ❋ Determine if any weaknesses or vulnerabilities exist in the encryption implementation that could aid in recovery or decryption.

6. Code Reconstruction:

   ❋ Reverse engineer the ransomware's code to gain a deeper understanding of its functionality and logic.

   ❋ Identify the entry points, key functions, and decision-making processes within the code.

   ❋ Reconstruct high-level code representations, such as pseudo-code or flowcharts, to facilitate analysis and visualization.

7. Malware Families and Variants:

   ❋ Compare the analyzed ransomware sample with known malware families and variants to determine its classification.

   ❋ Consult threat intelligence sources and cybersecurity communities to identify similar samples or related campaigns.

   ❋ Identify any unique characteristics or modifications made by the ransomware authors that differentiate it from other variants.

8. IOCs and Mitigation:

   ❋ Extract indicators of compromise (IOCs) from the analyzed ransomware, including file hashes, domain names, IP addresses, or URLs used by the ransomware.

- Share the IOCs with relevant cybersecurity organizations, industry peers, or threat intelligence platforms to aid in detection and mitigation efforts.
- Develop and update detection signatures, rules, or policies based on the identified IOCs to enhance defense capabilities.

9. Post-Infection Analysis:
   - Analyze the impact of the ransomware on the infected systems or networks.
   - Identify the files encrypted, file extensions used, and the ransom note left by the attackers.
   - Assess the effectiveness of the ransomware's encryption and the feasibility of recovering encrypted files.
10. Collaboration and Information Sharing:
   - Engage in information sharing initiatives and collaborate with the cybersecurity community to exchange insights, share findings, and develop effective countermeasures against ransomware.
   - Stay updated with the latest research, analysis, and trends related to ransomware to enhance analysis capabilities and response strategies.

By conducting comprehensive analysis of ransomware, organizations and cybersecurity professionals can gain valuable insights into its behavior, propagation methods, and potential mitigations. This knowledge enables them to develop effective defense strategies, enhance incident response plans, and prevent or minimize the impact of ransomware attacks.

10.2 EXAMINING BANKING TROJANS

Banking trojans are a type of malware specifically designed to target online banking and financial systems. They aim to steal sensitive financial information, such as login credentials, credit card details, or banking authentication codes. Analyzing banking trojans is crucial for understanding their tactics, techniques, and impact. Here are key aspects to consider when examining banking trojans:

1. Sample Acquisition:

   * Obtain a sample of the banking trojan for analysis. This can be done through controlled environments, malware repositories, or collaboration with cybersecurity organizations.

   * Ensure proper precautions are taken to handle the sample securely and prevent unintended infections or data loss.

2. Static Analysis:

   * Conduct static analysis by examining the trojan's code, structure, and other attributes without executing it.

   * Disassemble the code to understand its logic, functions, and potential obfuscation techniques.

   * Identify any encryption mechanisms, communication protocols, or evasion methods used by the trojan.

3. Dynamic Analysis:

   * Execute the banking trojan sample in a controlled environment, such as a virtual machine or sandbox, to observe its behavior.

   * Monitor system activities, network traffic, process creations, and registry modifications during execution.

   * Document and analyze the trojan's activities, such as keystroke logging, web injections, or form grabbing techniques.

4. Network Traffic Analysis:

   * Analyze network traffic generated by the trojan to identify communication patterns and potential command and control (C2) infrastructure.

   * Use network analysis tools to capture and inspect network packets for any indicators of compromise (IOCs) or malicious behavior.

   * Determine the communication protocols used by the trojan and extract any relevant data or configuration information.

5. Web Injection Analysis:

    * Focus on web injection techniques used by banking trojans to modify the content of online banking websites.

    * Analyze the injected code or HTML modifications to understand how the trojan captures user credentials or performs fraudulent transactions.

    * Identify the targets, injection triggers, and injection mechanisms employed by the trojan.

6. Malware Families and Variants:

    * Compare the analyzed banking trojan sample with known malware families and variants to determine its classification.

    * Consult threat intelligence sources and cybersecurity communities to identify similar samples or related campaigns.

    * Look for unique features or modifications made by the trojan authors that differentiate it from other variants.

7. Data Exfiltration:

    * Investigate how the trojan exfiltrates stolen data, such as login credentials or financial information.

    * Analyze the exfiltration mechanisms, encryption techniques, or data formats used by the trojan.

    * Determine the destination of the exfiltrated data and the potential impact on affected users or financial institutions.

8. Mitigation and Detection:

    * Extract indicators of compromise (IOCs) from the analyzed banking trojan, such as file hashes, domain names, IP addresses, or URLs used by the trojan.

    * Share the IOCs with relevant cybersecurity organizations, industry peers, or threat intelligence platforms to aid in detection and mitigation efforts.

    * Develop and update detection signatures, rules, or policies based on the identified IOCs to enhance defense capabilities.

9. Behavioral Analysis:

   * Analyze the trojan's behavior, such as its persistence mechanisms, evasion techniques, or anti-analysis capabilities.

   * Investigate any anti-sandbox or anti-debugging techniques employed by the trojan to evade detection.

   * Identify any modifications made to the system, registry, or processes by the trojan to maintain persistence and avoid removal.

10. Collaboration and Information Sharing:

    * Engage in information sharing initiatives and collaborate with the cybersecurity community to exchange insights, share findings, and develop effective countermeasures against banking trojans.

    * Stay updated with the latest research, analysis, and trends related to banking trojans to enhance analysis capabilities and response strategies.

By conducting thorough analysis of banking trojans, organizations and cybersecurity professionals can gain valuable insights into their techniques, modus operandi, and potential mitigations. This knowledge helps in developing robust security measures, enhancing incident response plans, and protecting online banking systems from these malicious threats.

10.3 REVERSE ENGINEERING ADVANCED PERSISTENT THREATS

Reverse engineering advanced persistent threats (APTs) is a complex and challenging task that involves analyzing sophisticated and persistent cyber threats targeting specific organizations or sectors. APTs often employ advanced techniques to evade detection and maintain long-term access to compromised systems. Here are key considerations when reverse engineering APTs:

1. Sample Acquisition:

   * Obtain a sample of the APT for analysis. This can be obtained through incident response investigations,

malware repositories, or collaboration with cybersecurity organizations.

* Ensure proper precautions are taken to handle the sample securely and prevent unintended infections or data loss.

2. Static Analysis:

* Conduct static analysis by examining the APT's code, structure, and other attributes without executing it.

* Disassemble the code to understand its logic, functions, and potential obfuscation techniques.

* Identify any anti-analysis or anti-reverse engineering measures employed by the APT.

3. Dynamic Analysis:

* Execute the APT sample in a controlled environment, such as a virtual machine or sandbox, to observe its behavior.

* Monitor system activities, network traffic, process creations, and registry modifications during execution.

* Document and analyze the APT's activities, including network communication, process injection, data exfiltration, or lateral movement techniques.

4. Persistence Mechanisms:

* Investigate the persistence mechanisms used by the APT to maintain long-term access to compromised systems.

* Analyze the techniques employed, such as modifying system registry keys, creating scheduled tasks, or utilizing rootkits.

* Identify any backdoor functionality or hidden components that enable the APT to maintain control over the compromised environment.

5. Command and Control (C2) Infrastructure:

* Analyze the APT's communication with its command and control infrastructure.

* Monitor network traffic and analyze network protocols used for communication.

* Determine the techniques employed to evade detection, such as domain generation algorithms (DGAs), encrypted communication channels, or use of legitimate services for communication.

6. Data Exfiltration and Encryption:

   * Investigate how the APT exfiltrates data from compromised systems.

   * Analyze the exfiltration techniques, encryption mechanisms, or data obfuscation methods employed by the APT.

   * Identify the data exfiltration channels, including network protocols, covert channels, or exfiltration through legitimate services.

7. Malware Families and Campaign Analysis:

   * Compare the analyzed APT sample with known APT groups, malware families, or previous campaigns to identify potential attribution or similarities.

   * Consult threat intelligence sources, cybersecurity communities, and research reports for information on similar APT activities.

   * Identify unique features, code similarities, or artifacts that may provide insights into the APT's origin or techniques.

8. Behavioral Analysis:

   * Analyze the APT's behavior to understand its objectives, techniques, and potential impact on the targeted organization.

   * Investigate any lateral movement, privilege escalation, or reconnaissance techniques employed by the APT to expand its presence within the network.

   * Identify any zero-day vulnerabilities or advanced exploitation techniques utilized by the APT.

9. Collaboration and Information Sharing:

   * Engage in information sharing initiatives and collaborate with the cybersecurity community, government agencies, or industry peers to exchange insights and share findings.

   * Participate in threat intelligence sharing platforms and communities to enhance knowledge about APTs and emerging threats.

   * Share analyzed APT samples, indicators of compromise (IOCs), or analysis reports to aid in the detection and mitigation of APT activities.

10. Continuous Learning and Adaptation:

    * Stay updated with the latest research, reports, and analysis related to APTs to enhance reverse engineering capabilities and response strategies.

    * Continuously improve analysis techniques, develop new tools, or utilize machine learning and artificial intelligence to enhance APT detection and analysis.

Reverse engineering APTs requires a combination of technical skills, experience, and access to relevant resources. By thoroughly analyzing APT samples, organizations and cybersecurity professionals can gain valuable insights into their techniques, motives, and potential mitigations. This knowledge helps in enhancing incident response capabilities, improving defense mechanisms, and developing countermeasures against persistent and sophisticated cyber threats.

10.4 ANALYSIS OF MOBILE MALWARE

The analysis of mobile malware is crucial for understanding the threats targeting mobile devices, such as smartphones and tablets. Mobile malware can compromise user privacy, steal sensitive information, perform unauthorized activities, or even gain control of the device. Here are key aspects to consider when analyzing mobile malware:

1. Sample Acquisition:

   ✳ Obtain a sample of the mobile malware for analysis. This can be obtained through controlled environments, app markets, or collaboration with cybersecurity organizations.

   ✳ Ensure proper precautions are taken to handle the sample securely and prevent unintended infections or data loss.

2. Static Analysis:

   ✳ Conduct static analysis by examining the malware's code, structure, and other attributes without executing it.

   ✳ Decompile the application or analyze the APK (Android) or IPA (iOS) files to understand the logic, functions, and potential obfuscation techniques.

   ✳ Identify any suspicious permissions, APIs, or embedded payloads within the malware.

3. Dynamic Analysis:

   ✳ Execute the mobile malware sample in a controlled environment, such as an emulator or sandbox, to observe its behavior.

   ✳ Monitor system activities, network traffic, file modifications, and registry changes during execution.

   ✳ Document and analyze the malware's activities, such as data exfiltration, command execution, or unauthorized communication.

4. Privacy and Data Leakage Analysis:

   ✳ Investigate how the mobile malware handles sensitive user data and privacy.

   ✳ Analyze permissions used by the malware and determine if they are excessive or unnecessary for the app's functionality.

   ✳ Identify data leakage or exfiltration techniques employed by the malware, such as unauthorized access to contacts, messages, or location data.

5. Network Traffic Analysis:

    ✻ Analyze network traffic generated by the mobile malware to identify communication patterns and potential command and control (C2) infrastructure.

    ✻ Use network analysis tools to capture and inspect network packets for any indicators of compromise (IOCs) or malicious behavior.

    ✻ Determine the communication protocols, encryption methods, or covert channels used by the malware.

6. Code Verification and Integrity:

    ✻ Verify the integrity of the mobile application's code and components to detect any modifications or tampering.

    ✻ Identify code injection techniques or malicious libraries used by the malware.

    ✻ Analyze the interaction between the legitimate and malicious components of the application.

7. Behavior Analysis:

    ✻ Analyze the behavior of the mobile malware to understand its objectives, functionality, and potential impact.

    ✻ Investigate any malicious activities performed by the malware, such as premium SMS sending, click fraud, ad fraud, or unauthorized device modifications.

    ✻ Identify any rootkit or jailbreak detection evasion techniques employed by the malware.

8. Malware Families and Variants:

    ✻ Compare the analyzed mobile malware sample with known malware families and variants to determine its classification.

    ✻ Consult threat intelligence sources, mobile security communities, and research reports for information on similar malware activities.

    ✻ Look for unique features, code similarities, or artifacts that may provide insights into the malware's origin or techniques.

9. Mitigation and Detection:

    ✱ Extract indicators of compromise (IOCs) from the analyzed mobile malware, such as package names, file hashes, URLs, or suspicious behaviors.

    ✱ Share the IOCs with relevant cybersecurity organizations, mobile app stores, or threat intelligence platforms to aid in detection and mitigation efforts.

    ✱ Develop and update detection signatures, rules, or policies based on the identified IOCs to enhance defense capabilities.

10. Collaboration and Information Sharing:

    ✱ Engage in information sharing initiatives and collaborate with the mobile security community, app developers, or cybersecurity organizations to exchange insights and share findings.

    ✱ Participate in mobile threat intelligence sharing platforms and communities to enhance knowledge about mobile malware and emerging threats.

    ✱ Share analyzed mobile malware samples, IOCs, or analysis reports to aid in the detection and mitigation of mobile malware activities.

Analyzing mobile malware requires specialized tools, knowledge of mobile operating systems, and an understanding of mobile app security. By conducting thorough analysis of mobile malware, organizations and cybersecurity professionals can gain valuable insights into their behavior, techniques, and potential mitigations. This knowledge helps in developing robust security measures, enhancing incident response capabilities, and protecting mobile devices from malicious threats.

Chapter 11

EMERGING TRENDS IN MALWARE ANALYSIS

Malware analysis is a constantly evolving field due to the ever-changing nature of cyber threats. Keeping up with emerging trends is crucial for staying ahead of cybercriminals and effectively analyzing new and sophisticated malware. Here are some emerging trends in malware analysis:

1. Fileless Malware Analysis:

   * Fileless malware operates in memory without leaving traditional traces on disk, making it harder to detect and analyze.

   * Emerging techniques focus on memory forensics, analyzing runtime behavior, and identifying malicious artifacts in volatile memory.

   * Advanced memory analysis tools and techniques help identify and analyze fileless malware, enabling effective detection and response.

2. Malware in Cloud Environments:

   * With the increasing adoption of cloud services, cybercriminals are targeting cloud environments with malware.

   * Malware analysis techniques are evolving to handle cloud-specific challenges, such as analyzing malicious cloud storage accounts, containerized environments, or serverless architectures.

* Cloud-based sandboxing and behavioral analysis tools are being developed to detect and analyze malware in cloud environments.

3. Evolving Evasion Techniques:

    * Malware authors constantly develop evasion techniques to bypass traditional detection mechanisms.

    * Emerging trends focus on identifying and analyzing evasion techniques, such as anti-VM, anti-sandbox, and anti-debugging techniques.

    * Enhanced emulation and dynamic analysis tools help researchers understand and counteract these evasion mechanisms.

4. IoT Malware Analysis:

    * The proliferation of Internet of Things (IoT) devices has led to the emergence of malware targeting these devices.

    * Malware analysis techniques are adapting to analyze IoT-specific malware, including firmware analysis, reverse engineering embedded systems, and analyzing network protocols used by IoT malware.

    * Specialized tools and methodologies are being developed to effectively analyze IoT malware and uncover its capabilities.

5. Machine Learning in Malware Analysis:

    * Machine learning techniques are increasingly being utilized to automate and improve various aspects of malware analysis.

    * ML algorithms help in identifying patterns, classifying malware samples, and detecting zero-day threats.

    * Advanced ML-based malware analysis platforms are being developed, enabling faster detection, better feature extraction, and behavior modeling.

6. Behavioral and Context-based Analysis:

    * Analyzing malware behavior in real-time and in context is gaining prominence.

✳ Behavioral analysis techniques focus on understanding the actions and intentions of malware during execution.

✳ Context-based analysis combines behavioral data with threat intelligence, network traffic analysis, and user behavior to identify and respond to advanced threats.

7. Collaboration and Threat Intelligence Sharing:

✳ Collaboration and sharing of threat intelligence among organizations, security vendors, and research communities are becoming essential for effective malware analysis.

✳ Platforms for sharing IOCs, malware samples, and analysis reports enable faster detection and response to emerging threats.

✳ Enhanced information sharing facilitates a proactive approach to malware analysis and helps identify broader attack campaigns and trends.

8. Automated Malware Analysis:

✳ The volume and complexity of malware require more efficient analysis techniques.

✳ Automated malware analysis platforms and frameworks are being developed to accelerate the analysis process and provide scalable solutions.

✳ Automated systems leverage sandboxing, machine learning, and behavior analysis to rapidly identify and classify malware.

By staying abreast of emerging trends in malware analysis, cybersecurity professionals can enhance their capabilities to detect, analyze, and respond to new and sophisticated malware threats. These trends reflect the evolving nature of cyber threats and the need for continuous improvement in malware analysis techniques and tools.

11.1 FILELESS MALWARE ANALYSIS

Fileless malware is a type of malware that operates entirely in memory, leaving little or no traditional traces on the victim's disk. Analyzing fileless malware presents unique challenges as it evades detection by traditional antivirus solutions and leaves minimal artifacts for analysis. Here are key considerations for fileless malware analysis:

1. Memory Forensics:

    * Fileless malware analysis heavily relies on memory forensics techniques.

    * Capture memory snapshots using specialized tools like Volatility or Rekall to preserve the state of the infected system for analysis.

    * Analyze the memory dump to identify running processes, injected code, and other malicious artifacts residing in memory.

2. Runtime Behavior Analysis:

    * Fileless malware operates in memory, making it essential to analyze its runtime behavior.

    * Monitor system activities, API calls, network connections, and registry modifications during the execution of the malware.

    * Tools like Process Monitor, API monitors, and network traffic analyzers help capture and analyze the dynamic behavior of fileless malware.

3. Endpoint Detection and Response (EDR) Tools:

    * EDR solutions provide real-time monitoring and detection capabilities for fileless malware.

    * Leverage EDR tools to capture telemetry data, including process behavior, memory access, and system events.

    * Analyze the EDR logs to identify suspicious or anomalous activities associated with fileless malware.

4. Memory Analysis Tools:

    * Use specialized memory analysis tools to dissect memory dumps and identify malicious code or injected payloads.

    * Tools like Volatility, Rekall, or DumpIt assist in extracting critical artifacts such as DLLs, injected code, or hidden processes from memory.

❊ Analyze the extracted artifacts to understand the malware's behavior, persistence mechanisms, and potential indicators of compromise.

5. Malicious Code Identification:

   ❊ Fileless malware often utilizes code injection techniques to execute malicious payloads in legitimate processes.

   ❊ Analyze the injected code or hooks within legitimate processes to identify the source and functionality of the malicious code.

   ❊ Understand the techniques employed, such as process hollowing, DLL injection, or direct code injection, to determine the extent of the compromise.

6. Network Traffic Analysis:

   ❊ Although fileless malware operates in memory, it may still establish network connections for communication or downloading additional payloads.

   ❊ Analyze network traffic logs, firewall logs, or packet captures to identify any suspicious or unauthorized communication associated with the fileless malware.

   ❊ Correlate network activity with memory analysis findings to gain a comprehensive understanding of the malware's activities.

7. Behavior-Based Detection:

   ❊ Fileless malware often exhibits distinct behavior patterns that can be used for detection.

   ❊ Employ behavior-based detection techniques, such as anomaly detection or heuristics, to identify unusual memory access, privilege escalation attempts, or suspicious API calls.

   ❊ Use endpoint security solutions that employ behavior-based detection mechanisms to identify fileless malware activities.

8. Advanced Threat Hunting:

   * Adopt proactive threat hunting techniques to detect and respond to fileless malware.

   * Continuously monitor and analyze system logs, memory dumps, and network traffic for signs of fileless malware activity.

   * Leverage threat intelligence feeds, IOCs, and knowledge of attacker tactics, techniques, and procedures (TTPs) to hunt for fileless malware in the environment.

9. Machine Learning and Artificial Intelligence:

   * Apply machine learning and AI algorithms to analyze memory behavior, identify anomalies, and detect fileless malware.

   * Develop models that can detect suspicious memory access patterns, unusual process behavior, or memory code injection techniques.

   * Train models using known fileless malware samples and continually update them to adapt to emerging threats.

10. Collaboration and Information Sharing:

   * Engage in collaborative efforts with the cybersecurity community, sharing findings, IOCs, and analysis techniques specific to fileless malware.

   * Contribute to threat intelligence platforms, sharing insights and knowledge to enhance the detection and analysis capabilities of fileless malware.

By employing specialized techniques, leveraging memory analysis tools, and adopting proactive detection strategies, analysts can effectively analyze fileless malware and detect its presence within an infected system. As fileless malware continues to evolve, ongoing research, collaboration, and the development of advanced analysis techniques are essential to staying ahead of these stealthy threats.

11.2 IoT MALWARE ANALYSIS

The rise of Internet of Things (IoT) devices has introduced new challenges for malware analysis. IoT malware specifically targets connected devices, such as smart home devices, industrial systems, or healthcare equipment. Analyzing IoT malware requires a unique approach due to the diversity of IoT architectures and communication protocols. Here are key considerations for IoT malware analysis:

1. Firmware Analysis:

    * IoT devices often run custom firmware that may contain vulnerabilities or malicious code.

    * Extract and analyze the firmware from the IoT device using tools like Binwalk or firmware extraction utilities.

    * Disassemble and decompile the firmware to understand its structure, identify embedded components, and locate potential malware payloads.

2. Reverse Engineering Embedded Systems:

    * IoT devices commonly use embedded systems with specialized architectures.

    * Analyze the hardware components, including microcontrollers, system-on-chips (SoCs), or field-programmable gate arrays (FPGAs), to understand their capabilities and potential vulnerabilities.

    * Reverse engineer the firmware's execution flow, identify relevant entry points, and analyze the interaction between hardware and software components.

3. Network Protocol Analysis:

    * Analyze the network protocols used by IoT devices to communicate with other devices or servers.

    * Capture network traffic between the IoT device and its associated infrastructure using tools like Wireshark or tcpdump.

    * Identify any anomalous or suspicious network behavior, such as unusual communication patterns or unauthorized data transfers.

4. Hardware Interfaces:

   ❋ Investigate the hardware interfaces exposed by IoT devices, such as USB, UART, JTAG, or SPI.

   ❋ Utilize appropriate hardware tools, such as logic analyzers or JTAG debuggers, to gain low-level access to the IoT device.

   ❋ Extract data, debug firmware, or analyze memory contents through hardware interfaces for deeper analysis.

5. Application Analysis:

   ❋ Analyze the IoT device's companion mobile or web application used for device management.

   ❋ Reverse engineer the application to identify potential vulnerabilities or insecure communication channels.

   ❋ Analyze the APIs and data exchanges between the application and the IoT device to understand potential attack vectors or exploitation opportunities.

6. Protocol Fuzzing:

   ❋ Conduct protocol fuzzing to identify potential vulnerabilities in IoT device communication protocols.

   ❋ Develop or utilize existing fuzzing frameworks to send malformed or unexpected data to the device and monitor its response.

   ❋ Analyze crash reports or abnormal behaviors to identify potential security weaknesses.

7. Behavior-Based Analysis:

   ❋ Focus on the behavior of the IoT device and monitor its activities in real-time.

   ❋ Set up an IoT honeypot or controlled environment to observe the device's behavior when interacting with malicious commands or network traffic.

   ❋ Monitor system logs, device outputs, or sensor readings to detect any anomalies or suspicious activities.

8. Threat Intelligence and Collaboration:

    *   Leverage threat intelligence feeds and collaborate with IoT security communities and research groups to stay updated on emerging IoT malware threats.

    *   Share findings, analysis techniques, and IOCs with the cybersecurity community to enhance collective defense against IoT malware.

    *   Engage in collaborative efforts to share insights and contribute to the development of open-source tools and frameworks for IoT malware analysis.

9. Emulation and Simulation:

    *   Utilize emulation or simulation platforms to recreate the IoT device's environment for analysis.

    *   Emulate the device's firmware, network behavior, and sensor outputs to observe the malware's activities without directly impacting a live environment.

    *   Analyze the malware's behavior, network interactions, and potential impact on the emulated IoT device.

10. Continuous Research and Adaptation:

    *   Keep up with the evolving landscape of IoT devices and associated malware threats.

    *   Stay updated on the latest research, vulnerabilities, and analysis techniques related to IoT malware.

    *   Continuously adapt and enhance analysis methodologies to address new attack vectors and emerging IoT malware trends.

By employing specialized techniques, collaborating with the IoT security community, and continuously adapting analysis methodologies, cybersecurity professionals can effectively analyze IoT malware and mitigate the risks associated with compromised IoT devices.

11.3 CLOUD-BASED MALWARE ANALYSIS

With the increasing adoption of cloud computing, malware threats targeting cloud environments have also emerged. Analyzing cloud-based malware requires specialized techniques to understand its behavior, detect malicious activities, and mitigate the risks. Here are key considerations for cloud-based malware analysis:

1. Cloud-Specific Challenges:

    ❋   Recognize the unique challenges of analyzing malware in a cloud environment.

    ❋   Understand the shared responsibility model between cloud service providers and users.

    ❋   Consider the security controls, logging capabilities, and access to metadata provided by the cloud platform.

2. Malware Sample Acquisition:

    ❋   Obtain a sample of the cloud-based malware for analysis.

    ❋   Securely acquire the sample from cloud storage, email attachments, or compromised instances.

    ❋   Follow proper protocols to prevent unintended infections or data leakage during acquisition.

3. Static Analysis:

    ❋   Conduct static analysis by examining the malware sample's code and structure.

    ❋   Disassemble or decompile the malware to understand its functionality and potential obfuscation techniques.

    ❋   Identify any suspicious or malicious artifacts embedded within the malware.

4. Dynamic Analysis:

    ❋   Execute the cloud-based malware sample in a controlled environment, such as a sandbox or virtual machine, to observe its behavior.

    ❋   Monitor system activities, network traffic, process executions, and API calls during the execution of the malware.

    ❋   Document and analyze the malware's activities, such as file modifications, network connections, or unauthorized access attempts.

5. Network Traffic Analysis:

    *   Analyze network traffic generated by the cloud-based malware to identify communication patterns and potential command and control (C2) infrastructure.

    *   Capture and inspect network packets using tools like Wireshark or cloud-native network analysis services.

    *   Identify any suspicious or unauthorized network connections, data exfiltration attempts, or communication with malicious IP addresses.

6. Cloud Storage Analysis:

    *   Investigate the use of cloud storage by the malware to store or retrieve malicious payloads or configuration data.

    *   Analyze cloud storage logs, access controls, and permissions to identify unauthorized or suspicious activities.

    *   Monitor for changes in the cloud storage containers, files, or permissions associated with the malware.

7. Behavioral Analysis:

    *   Focus on the behavior of the cloud-based malware to understand its objectives and potential impact.

    *   Analyze its persistence mechanisms, evasion techniques, or anti-analysis capabilities.

    *   Identify any modifications made to cloud resources, APIs, or configurations by the malware.

8. Memory Analysis:

    *   Analyze memory artifacts of cloud instances or containers where the malware is executed.

    *   Capture memory snapshots or utilize cloud-native memory analysis tools to extract relevant artifacts.

    *   Investigate the presence of injected code, malicious processes, or runtime modifications in the memory.

9. Log Analysis:

   ✳ Leverage cloud logs and auditing features to identify indicators of compromise (IOCs) and malicious activities.

   ✳ Analyze logs related to identity and access management, network traffic, resource provisioning, and system events.

   ✳ Correlate log data with other analysis findings to uncover the malware's activities and persistence mechanisms.

10. Collaboration and Threat Intelligence:

   ✳ Engage in collaboration with cloud service providers, cybersecurity communities, and threat intelligence platforms to exchange insights and IOCs related to cloud-based malware.

   ✳ Share analysis findings, techniques, and countermeasures to enhance the collective defense against cloud-based malware.

   ✳ Stay updated with emerging threats, vulnerabilities, and security best practices specific to cloud environments.

11. Compliance and Incident Response Considerations:

   ✳ Comply with legal and regulatory requirements regarding incident response and data protection in the cloud environment.

   ✳ Document the analysis process, findings, and remediation steps for compliance purposes.

   ✳ Integrate cloud-based malware analysis within an incident response framework to ensure effective detection, containment, and recovery.

Analyzing cloud-based malware requires expertise in cloud security, knowledge of cloud service provider capabilities, and familiarity with cloud-native analysis tools. By employing specialized techniques, leveraging cloud platform features, and collaborating with the cybersecurity community, analysts can effectively detect, analyze, and respond to malware threats targeting cloud environments.

11.4 ARTIFICIAL INTELLIGENCE IN MALWARE ANALYSIS

Artificial intelligence (AI) is increasingly being applied in malware analysis to enhance detection capabilities, automate analysis processes, and improve overall cybersecurity. AI techniques enable the analysis of large volumes of malware samples, detection of previously unknown threats, and identification of advanced malware behaviors. Here are key aspects of using AI in malware analysis:

1. Machine Learning-Based Malware Detection:

    * Machine learning algorithms can learn from vast datasets of known malware samples to identify patterns and characteristics that distinguish malware from benign software.

    * Train machine learning models using features extracted from malware samples, such as file attributes, API calls, or code sequences.

    * Apply these trained models to classify new or unknown samples as either malicious or benign.

2. Behavioral Analysis:

    * AI-based approaches enable the analysis of malware behavior by monitoring and modeling system activities, network traffic, or process execution.

    * Employ machine learning algorithms to detect anomalies or malicious behaviors that deviate from expected norms.

    * Use behavioral analysis to identify zero-day malware or sophisticated evasion techniques.

3. Automated Feature Extraction:

    * AI algorithms can automatically extract relevant features from malware samples, reducing the manual effort required for feature engineering.

    * Extract features such as opcode sequences, system calls, or byte-level n-grams, which capture unique characteristics of malware.

* Feature extraction algorithms can adapt and evolve based on the changing landscape of malware threats.

4. Deep Learning for Malware Analysis:

* Deep learning, a subset of machine learning, employs neural networks with multiple layers to learn complex patterns and relationships in data.

* Apply deep learning models, such as convolutional neural networks (CNNs) or recurrent neural networks (RNNs), to analyze malware samples.

* Deep learning models can detect subtle variations in malware behavior or identify hidden patterns that may not be easily captured by traditional approaches.

5. Threat Intelligence and Adversarial Machine Learning:

* Utilize AI techniques to analyze large-scale threat intelligence data, including malware samples, network traffic, or security logs.

* Apply adversarial machine learning to detect and mitigate adversarial attacks, where malware authors attempt to bypass traditional defenses.

* Adversarial machine learning helps improve the robustness of malware detection models against evasion techniques.

6. Malware Variant and Family Detection:

* AI algorithms can analyze similarities and differences across malware samples to group them into families or detect variants of known malware.

* Use clustering algorithms, similarity measures, or graph-based techniques to identify relationships and hierarchical structures among malware samples.

* AI-based malware clustering facilitates faster and more efficient analysis of large malware datasets.

7. Exploit and Vulnerability Analysis:

* Apply AI techniques to analyze vulnerabilities and potential exploit techniques used by malware.

✳ Employ natural language processing (NLP) algorithms to process security advisories, vulnerability databases, or research papers to extract relevant information.

✳ Use AI-driven vulnerability analysis to identify potential weaknesses in software or systems targeted by malware.

8. Malware Generation and Defense:

   ✳ AI can be utilized to generate synthetic malware samples for testing and evaluating security defenses.

   ✳ Adversarial machine learning techniques enable the creation of robust defenses against new and evolving malware threats.

   ✳ AI-based defenses can adapt and learn from incoming threats, improving the overall resilience of security systems.

9. Human-Machine Collaboration:

   ✳ AI augments human expertise in malware analysis by automating time-consuming tasks, increasing efficiency, and providing valuable insights.

   ✳ Analysts can focus on higher-level analysis, investigating complex behaviors, and validating AI-generated results.

   ✳ Human expertise complements AI capabilities, ensuring the accuracy and context-awareness of analysis results.

10. Continuous Learning and Adaptation:

   ✳ AI models and algorithms need to be continually updated and trained to keep pace with evolving malware threats.

   ✳ Regularly retrain machine learning models with new datasets, incorporating the latest malware samples and features.

   ✳ Stay updated with the latest research and developments in AI-driven malware analysis to enhance analysis capabilities.

AI-based approaches in malware analysis have the potential to improve detection accuracy, reduce false positives, and enhance overall cybersecurity defenses. By leveraging AI techniques, cybersecurity professionals can efficiently analyze and respond to the increasing volume and complexity of malware threats. Continuous research, collaboration, and integration of AI technologies are key to harnessing its full potential in malware analysis.

Chapter 12
BEST PRACTICES AND PRACTICAL TIPS

Malware analysis requires a systematic and meticulous approach to ensure accurate results and effective mitigation of threats. Here are some best practices and practical tips to enhance your malware analysis process:

1. Establish a Controlled Environment:

    * Create a controlled and isolated environment for malware analysis, such as a virtual machine or sandbox, to prevent malware from infecting the host system.

    * Use separate network segments or VLANs to isolate the malware analysis environment from the production network.

2. Document and Preserve Evidence:

    * Maintain a detailed record of the entire analysis process, including sample acquisition, analysis techniques employed, and findings.

    * Capture screenshots, record system activities, and document any observed behaviors or artifacts.

    * Preserve the original malware sample and any associated files for further analysis or legal purposes.

3. Use Multiple Analysis Techniques:

    * Employ a combination of static and dynamic analysis techniques to gain a comprehensive understanding of the malware's behavior and characteristics.

* Use a variety of tools, such as disassemblers, debuggers, network analyzers, and behavior analysis platforms, to extract maximum information from the malware sample.

4. Leverage Open-Source Tools and Frameworks:

   * Take advantage of open-source malware analysis tools, such as IDA Pro, OllyDbg, Wireshark, or Cuckoo Sandbox, to enhance your analysis capabilities.

   * Participate in the open-source community to contribute to existing tools, share insights, and collaborate with other analysts.

5. Stay Updated with Threat Intelligence:

   * Regularly monitor threat intelligence feeds, security blogs, and research papers to stay informed about the latest malware trends, vulnerabilities, and analysis techniques.

   * Subscribe to mailing lists or join forums dedicated to malware analysis to engage with the community and share knowledge.

6. Validate Findings with Multiple Sources:

   * Verify your analysis findings and indicators of compromise (IOCs) by cross-referencing with other trusted sources, such as antivirus vendors, malware repositories, or threat intelligence platforms.

   * Collaborate with other analysts or teams to validate your analysis results and ensure accuracy.

7. Develop Indicators of Compromise (IOCs):

   * Extract IOCs, such as file hashes, IP addresses, domain names, or registry keys, from the malware sample to aid in detection and mitigation efforts.

   * Share IOCs with relevant stakeholders, such as internal security teams, antivirus vendors, or threat intelligence platforms, to enhance the collective defense against malware.

8. Collaborate and Share Insights:

    * Engage in information sharing initiatives, both within your organization and with external entities, to exchange insights, analysis techniques, and IOCs.

    * Join or participate in malware analysis communities, forums, or mailing lists to share experiences, seek assistance, and contribute to the broader cybersecurity community.

9. Practice Safe Handling of Malware Samples:

    * Handle malware samples with caution to prevent accidental infections or unauthorized dissemination.

    * Use dedicated and isolated systems or virtual machines for sample analysis.

    * Implement strict access controls and securely store malware samples to prevent unauthorized access.

10. Continuous Learning and Professional Development:

    * Stay curious and continuously update your knowledge and skills in malware analysis.

    * Attend cybersecurity conferences, webinars, or training programs to learn about the latest analysis techniques, tools, and emerging threats.

    * Engage in hands-on practice and conduct personal research to hone your expertise.

11. Follow Legal and Ethical Guidelines:

    * Adhere to legal and ethical guidelines when performing malware analysis.

    * Obtain proper permissions and consent for sample acquisition and analysis.

    * Respect privacy rights and ensure the secure handling of sensitive information encountered during the analysis process.

12. Backup and Recovery:

* Regularly back up critical systems and data to ensure quick recovery in case of malware infections or accidental system disruptions during the analysis process.

* Test the backup and recovery process to validate its effectiveness and reliability.

By following these best practices and practical tips, you can enhance the efficiency and accuracy of your malware analysis efforts, mitigate risks effectively, and contribute to the overall security of your organization and the broader cybersecurity community.

12.1 MALWARE ANALYSIS WORKFLOW

A well-defined malware analysis workflow helps ensure a systematic and consistent approach to analyzing and understanding malware. While the specific steps and techniques may vary depending on the situation and resources available, here is a general malware analysis workflow to guide you:

1. Step 1: Sample Acquisition and Documentation

* Obtain the malware sample from a trusted source or infected system.

* Document relevant information, such as the source of the sample, acquisition date, and any associated details.

2. Step 2: Preliminary Analysis

* Perform initial checks to gather basic information about the malware sample without executing it.

* Examine file properties, such as file size, file type, and metadata, to gain initial insights.

3. Step 3: Static Analysis

* Conduct static analysis by examining the malware sample's code and structure without executing it.

* Use disassemblers, decompilers, or static analysis tools to understand the functionality, logic, and potential obfuscation techniques used by the malware.

✳   Identify potential indicators of compromise (IOCs) such as file names, registry keys, or embedded URLs.

4. Step 4: Dynamic Analysis

   ✳   Execute the malware sample in a controlled environment, such as a virtual machine or sandbox, to observe its behavior.

   ✳   Monitor system activities, network traffic, and API calls during the execution of the malware.

   ✳   Analyze any modifications made to files, registry entries, or network connections by the malware.

5. Step 5: Behavioral Analysis

   ✳   Focus on understanding the behavior and actions of the malware during dynamic analysis.

   ✳   Observe system interactions, file access patterns, process creation, and network communication to identify malicious activities.

   ✳   Document observed behaviors and their potential impact on the infected system.

6. Step 6: Code and Memory Analysis

   ✳   Dive deeper into the malware's code and memory to identify additional functionality and potential vulnerabilities.

   ✳   Use disassemblers, debuggers, or memory analysis tools to analyze the malware's code execution flow, identify injected code, or analyze memory artifacts.

   ✳   Examine API calls, function calls, and code logic to understand the malware's functionality and potential evasion techniques.

7. Step 7: Network Traffic Analysis

   ✳   Analyze network traffic generated by the malware to identify communication channels, command and control (C2) infrastructure, or data exfiltration attempts.

   ✳   Capture and inspect network packets using tools like Wireshark or network traffic analysis platforms.

* Identify any suspicious or unauthorized network connections, protocols, or data transfers.

8. Step 8: Post-Analysis Documentation and Reporting

   * Document the analysis findings, including the observed behaviors, IOCs, and potential impact of the malware.

   * Prepare a detailed report summarizing the analysis process, key findings, and recommendations for remediation and mitigation.

   * Share the report with relevant stakeholders, such as incident response teams, IT administrators, or management.

9. Step 9: Indicators of Compromise (IOCs) Sharing

   * Extract IOCs from the analysis findings, such as file hashes, IP addresses, domain names, or registry keys.

   * Share the IOCs with relevant security communities, threat intelligence platforms, or internal security teams to enhance the collective defense against similar malware.

10. Step 10: Remediation and Mitigation

    * Develop a remediation plan based on the analysis findings to remove the malware and address any vulnerabilities or weaknesses identified.

    * Apply security patches, update antivirus signatures, or implement network access controls to prevent further infections.

    * Monitor the environment for any potential re-infections or signs of similar malware activities.

It's important to note that malware analysis is an iterative process, and additional steps or techniques may be required depending on the complexity of the malware and the specific goals of the analysis. Regularly update your analysis workflow based on new insights, emerging threats, and evolving analysis techniques to ensure effective malware analysis and mitigation.

12.2 DOCUMENTATION AND REPORTING IN MALWARE ANALYSIS

Documentation and reporting are crucial components of the malware analysis process. They help capture the analysis findings, provide insights to stakeholders, and facilitate future reference. Here are key considerations for effective documentation and reporting in malware analysis:

1. Detailed Analysis Notes:

   * Maintain detailed notes throughout the analysis process, documenting each step, technique used, and observed behaviors.

   * Record the timestamps of significant events, such as file modifications, network connections, or process creations.

   * Document any observed anomalies, evasion techniques, or potential indicators of compromise (IOCs).

2. Clear and Structured Reporting:

   * Prepare a comprehensive report summarizing the analysis process, key findings, and recommendations for mitigation and remediation.

   * Structure the report with clear sections for easy navigation and understanding.

   * Use appropriate headings, subheadings, and bullet points to present information in a concise and organized manner.

3. Executive Summary:

   * Include an executive summary at the beginning of the report to provide a high-level overview of the analysis findings, impact, and recommended actions.

   * Summarize the key points in a concise manner for non-technical stakeholders or decision-makers.

4. Analysis Methodology:

   * Describe the methodology used during the analysis, including the techniques, tools, and environments employed.

    ✳   Provide a step-by-step breakdown of the analysis process, highlighting the rationale behind each step.

    ✳   Include information on the sample acquisition process and any precautions taken to ensure safe handling.

5. Malware Description:

    ✳   Provide a detailed description of the malware, including its characteristics, functionality, and potential impact on the infected system or network.

    ✳   Describe the malware's propagation mechanisms, persistence methods, and any unique features or obfuscation techniques employed.

6. Behavioral Analysis Findings:

    ✳   Document the observed behaviors and activities of the malware during dynamic analysis.

    ✳   Include information on file modifications, registry changes, network connections, and any malicious actions taken by the malware.

    ✳   Analyze the potential implications of these behaviors on the compromised system or network.

7. IOCs and Indicators of Compromise:

    ✳   Compile a list of IOCs discovered during the analysis, such as file hashes, IP addresses, domain names, or registry keys.

    ✳   Provide detailed information on each IOC, including its significance, associated malware functionality, and recommendations for detection and mitigation.

8. Recommendations for Mitigation and Remediation:

    ✳   Offer actionable recommendations to mitigate the impact of the malware and prevent future infections.

    ✳   Suggest specific steps, such as applying security patches, updating antivirus signatures, or implementing network access controls.

    ✳   Provide guidance on incident response procedures, including steps for containment, eradication, and recovery.

9. Technical Appendices:

   * Include technical appendices, if necessary, to provide additional information or analysis artifacts that support the findings.

   * Appendices may include disassembly listings, memory dump analysis, network traffic captures, or relevant code snippets.

10. Clear and Concise Language:

    * Use clear and concise language to ensure the report is easily understandable by both technical and non-technical stakeholders.

    * Avoid jargon or technical terms without providing appropriate explanations.

    * Provide context and explanations for any specialized techniques or concepts mentioned.

11. Consider Target Audience:

    * Tailor the report to the specific needs and knowledge level of the intended audience.

    * Include additional sections or explanations for non-technical stakeholders, while providing sufficient technical details for security experts or incident responders.

12. Regular Updates and Version Control:

    * Maintain a consistent version control system for the report to track updates and revisions.

    * Ensure the report is regularly updated with new information or analysis findings as the investigation progresses.

    * Clearly mark the report with the analysis date and any subsequent updates or revisions.

Effective documentation and reporting enable knowledge sharing, facilitate incident response, and enhance the overall security posture of an organization. By following these best practices, you can produce clear, informative, and actionable reports that effectively communicate the findings of your malware analysis.

12.3 STAYING UPDATED AND CONTINUOUS LEARNING IN MALWARE ANALYSIS

Staying updated and continuously learning are essential practices for effective malware analysis. The field of cybersecurity and malware threats evolve rapidly, requiring analysts to keep up with the latest techniques, tools, and trends. Here are some strategies to stay updated and continue learning in malware analysis:

1. Engage in Continuous Education:

    * Attend relevant training courses, workshops, or webinars offered by reputable organizations, industry conferences, or cybersecurity training providers.

    * Participate in online courses or certification programs focused on malware analysis, reverse engineering, or incident response.

    * Stay updated with the latest research papers, whitepapers, and publications in the field of malware analysis.

2. Join Malware Analysis Communities:

    * Join online forums, mailing lists, or social media groups dedicated to malware analysis and cybersecurity.

    * Engage in discussions, ask questions, and share insights with fellow analysts and experts in the community.

    * Follow blogs or podcasts by respected cybersecurity researchers or malware analysts.

3. Participate in Capture the Flag (CTF) Challenges:

    * Take part in malware analysis Capture the Flag (CTF) challenges or competitions.

    * CTF challenges provide hands-on experience in analyzing real-world malware samples and solving related puzzles or challenges.

    * CTF challenges also offer an opportunity to learn from other participants and showcase your skills.

4. Follow Industry Experts and Thought Leaders:

    ✳ Follow industry experts, cybersecurity researchers, and thought leaders on social media platforms like Twitter or LinkedIn.

    ✳ Subscribe to their blogs or newsletters to receive updates on the latest malware trends, analysis techniques, and research findings.

    ✳ Attend webinars or live streams hosted by experts to gain insights and stay informed.

5. Read Security Reports and Threat Intelligence:

    ✳ Stay updated with security reports and threat intelligence feeds from reputable sources, such as security vendors, research organizations, or cybersecurity communities.

    ✳ These reports provide insights into the latest malware campaigns, attack techniques, and emerging threats.

    ✳ Analyze the reported incidents, malware samples, and analysis techniques mentioned in these reports.

6. Experiment with New Tools and Techniques:

    ✳ Explore new tools and techniques in malware analysis to expand your skill set and stay current with industry advancements.

    ✳ Experiment with open-source tools, frameworks, or scripts developed by the cybersecurity community.

    ✳ Stay updated with the latest features and updates in popular analysis tools and platforms.

7. Set Up a Malware Analysis Lab:

    ✳ Create a personal malware analysis lab with virtual machines, sandboxes, or dedicated hardware.

    ✳ Use the lab environment to practice and experiment with different analysis techniques, tools, and malware samples.

    ✳ Conduct hands-on experiments to deepen your understanding of malware behavior and evasion techniques.

8. Network and Collaborate:

   * Connect with fellow malware analysts, incident responders, and cybersecurity professionals through professional networks, conferences, or online communities.

   * Collaborate on research projects, share insights, and exchange knowledge to enhance your skills and expand your professional network.

9. Follow Malware Conferences and Webinars:

   * Stay updated on upcoming malware conferences, workshops, or webinars.

   * Attend or participate in these events to learn from industry experts, researchers, and practitioners.

   * Take note of the latest research presentations, case studies, and emerging techniques discussed during these events.

10. Document Your Findings and Lessons Learned:

   * Maintain a personal repository or knowledge base of your analysis findings, techniques, and lessons learned.

   * Document challenges you encounter, solutions you discover, and successful analysis methodologies for future reference.

   * Share your insights and lessons learned through blog posts, technical articles, or presentations to contribute to the broader cybersecurity community.

Remember, malware analysis is a constantly evolving field, and staying updated requires ongoing dedication to learning and exploring new techniques. Continuously expanding your knowledge and skills will enable you to effectively analyze and respond to emerging malware threats, ultimately enhancing your effectiveness as a malware analyst.

CONCLUSION

Malware analysis is a critical process in the field of cybersecurity, enabling analysts to understand the behavior, impact, and mitigation strategies for malicious software. This book has provided a comprehensive overview of malware analysis, covering various aspects such as the fundamentals of malware, analysis methodologies, detection techniques, and mitigation strategies. It has explored both static and dynamic analysis approaches, as well as the use of specialized tools and technologies.

The book emphasized the importance of setting up a proper malware analysis environment, including isolated testing environments, virtual machines, and sandboxes. It delved into the details of static analysis, examining file structures, metadata, and reverse engineering techniques. Dynamic analysis, including behavioral analysis, network traffic analysis, and system monitoring, was also explored in depth. Additionally, the book discussed advanced topics such as malware deobfuscation, reverse engineering, and the analysis of mobile malware.

Furthermore, the book highlighted the significance of staying updated with emerging trends in malware analysis, such as fileless malware, IoT malware, cloud-based malware, and the integration of artificial intelligence. It provided insights into incident response and mitigation strategies, emphasizing the importance of collaboration, documentation, and continuous learning.

By following the best practices outlined in this book, malware analysts can enhance their skills and knowledge, improve their analysis capabilities, and contribute to a stronger cybersecurity posture. However, it is crucial to remember that the field of malware analysis is ever-evolving, requiring continuous adaptation, learning, and collaboration to stay ahead of emerging threats.

With a solid understanding of malware analysis principles, practical techniques, and ethical considerations, analysts can effectively analyze and mitigate malware incidents, protect critical systems, and contribute to the overall security of organizations and individuals. By combining expertise, tools, and a proactive mindset, analysts play a vital role in safeguarding against the constantly evolving landscape of malware threats.

APPENDIX A: MALWARE ANALYSIS TOOLS

The field of malware analysis relies on a variety of specialized tools and technologies to assist analysts in dissecting and understanding malicious software. Here are some commonly used malware analysis tools:

1. Static Analysis Tools:

   * IDA Pro: A powerful disassembler and debugger used for analyzing and reverse engineering executable files.

   * Ghidra: An open-source software reverse engineering framework developed by the National Security Agency (NSA).

   * Binary Ninja: A modern and extensible binary analysis platform that offers a range of features for static analysis.

   * Radare2: A command-line framework for reverse engineering and analyzing binary files.

2. Dynamic Analysis Tools:

   * Cuckoo Sandbox: An open-source automated dynamic analysis system for analyzing suspicious files and monitoring their behavior.

   * Wireshark: A network protocol analyzer that captures and analyzes network traffic to observe malware communication.

   * Process Monitor: A Windows-based tool that monitors system activities, including file system, registry, and process events.

❋ Sysinternals Suite: A collection of advanced Windows system utilities, including tools like Process Explorer and Autoruns, which aid in analyzing running processes and autostart entries.

3. Sandboxing Tools:

❋ FireEye Sandbox: A commercial sandboxing solution that provides an isolated environment for executing and analyzing malware samples.

❋ Cuckoo Sandbox: As mentioned earlier, Cuckoo Sandbox also offers sandboxing capabilities for dynamic analysis.

❋ VMRay Analyzer: A malware analysis platform that combines dynamic analysis with advanced behavior-based monitoring and threat intelligence.

4. Network Traffic Analysis Tools:

❋ Bro/Zeek: An open-source network security monitoring platform that captures and analyzes network traffic for detecting and analyzing malware.

❋ Suricata: An open-source intrusion detection and prevention system that can be used for analyzing network traffic and identifying malicious activities.

❋ NetworkMiner: A network forensic analysis tool that captures and parses network packets to extract information and analyze potential malware-related activities.

5. Memory Analysis Tools:

❋ Volatility: An open-source framework for analyzing volatile memory (RAM) for detecting malware artifacts, such as processes, network connections, or injected code.

❋ Rekall: An advanced memory forensics framework that enables the analysis of physical and virtual memory for detecting malware-related artifacts.

❋ WinDbg: A Windows debugger that can be used for live kernel debugging and analyzing memory dumps.

6. Malware Sandboxes and Threat Intelligence Platforms:

   ✱ VirusTotal: An online service that analyzes suspicious files and URLs using multiple antivirus engines and various other detection techniques.

   ✱ Hybrid Analysis: A cloud-based malware analysis platform that combines static and dynamic analysis techniques to provide detailed reports on malware samples.

   ✱ Joe Sandbox: A comprehensive malware analysis platform that offers static and dynamic analysis, behavior monitoring, and threat intelligence integration.

These tools represent a small sample of the wide range of available options for malware analysis. Analysts should select tools based on their specific requirements, the type of malware being analyzed, and their level of expertise. It is also important to stay updated with the latest versions and releases of these tools, as they are constantly evolving to address emerging threats and enhance analysis capabilities.

APPENDIX A.2: MALWARE ANALYSIS TOOLS

Continuing from Appendix A, here are additional commonly used malware analysis tools:

1. Debuggers:

   ✱ OllyDbg: A popular and powerful debugger for analyzing Windows executables, allowing step-by-step code execution and memory inspection.

   ✱ WinDbg: A debugger provided by Microsoft that is commonly used for analyzing Windows kernel-mode components and system-level malware.

2. Sandboxing and Virtualization Tools:

   ✱ VMware Workstation: A virtualization software that allows the creation and management of virtual machines for malware analysis.

   ✱ VirtualBox: An open-source virtualization platform that enables the setup of virtual machines for analyzing malware in isolated environments.

✳ QEMU: A versatile virtualization framework that provides emulation and virtual machine support for malware analysis.

3. Memory Analysis Frameworks:

✳ Volatility Framework: An open-source framework designed for analyzing memory dumps to extract information about processes, network connections, and malware artifacts.

✳ Rekall: A memory forensics framework that facilitates the examination of volatile memory for detecting and analyzing malware.

4. Behavior Monitoring Tools:

✳ Sysmon: A Windows system service that monitors and logs system activity, including process creation, file modification, and network connections, helping in the detection of suspicious behaviors.

✳ OSSEC: An open-source host intrusion detection system that provides real-time monitoring and analysis of system logs for identifying potential malicious activities.

5. Malware Traffic Analysis Tools:

✳ Maltego: A powerful tool for analyzing and visualizing network traffic, domain information, and other intelligence sources to uncover relationships and connections related to malware.

✳ NetworkMiner: A network forensic analysis tool that captures and analyzes network traffic, extracting files, emails, and other artifacts related to malware.

6. File Analysis Tools:

✳ PEStudio: A tool for analyzing Windows executable files (PE files) to identify potential malware characteristics, such as suspicious imports, packed sections, or obfuscation techniques.

✳ OfficeMalScanner: A tool for analyzing Microsoft Office documents (Word, Excel, PowerPoint) to detect potential malicious macros or embedded malware.

7. Malware Repository and Threat Intelligence Platforms:

    *   MalwareBazaar: A public repository for sharing and accessing malware samples, providing a valuable resource for research and analysis.

    *   ThreatConnect: A threat intelligence platform that aggregates and analyzes data from various sources to provide insights into malware campaigns, indicators of compromise (IOCs), and associated threat actors.

These tools, along with those mentioned in Appendix A, form a comprehensive toolkit for malware analysis. It is important for analysts to select the appropriate tools based on their specific requirements, the type of malware being analyzed, and their level of expertise. Regularly exploring new tools, keeping up with updates, and staying informed about emerging technologies and techniques are essential for effective and efficient malware analysis.

APPENDIX A.3: MALWARE ANALYSIS TOOLS

Continuing from Appendices A and A.2, here are additional widely used tools in the field of malware analysis:

1. Sandboxing and Virtualization Tools:

    *   Sandboxie: A sandboxing tool that isolates applications from the underlying system, allowing for the safe execution and analysis of potentially malicious files.

    *   Firejail: A Linux-based sandboxing tool that provides a secure environment for running applications and isolating them from the host system.

2. Behavior Analysis Tools:

    *   Process Explorer: A Windows-based tool that provides detailed information about running processes, including their associated DLLs, network connections, and open files.

    *   API Monitor: A tool for monitoring and analyzing API calls made by applications, allowing for the identification of potentially malicious behavior.

3. Network Traffic Analysis Tools:

   ✳ Bro/Zeek: An open-source network security monitoring tool that captures and analyzes network traffic to detect and identify malicious activities.

   ✳ Security Onion: A Linux distribution that combines various network security monitoring and analysis tools, including Bro/Zeek, Suricata, and Wireshark.

4. YARA:

   ✳ YARA is a powerful pattern-matching tool used for identifying and classifying malware samples based on defined rules. It enables the creation of custom rules to detect specific patterns or characteristics of malware.

5. Reverse Engineering Tools:

   ✳ Radare2 Cutter: A user-friendly graphical interface for the Radare2 reverse engineering framework, providing a visual environment for analyzing binaries.

   ✳ Hopper: A macOS and Linux disassembler and decompiler that allows for interactive analysis and reverse engineering of executables.

6. Memory Analysis Tools:

   ✳ WinDbg with PyKD: A combination of the WinDbg debugger and the PyKD extension, allowing for the analysis of Windows memory dumps using Python scripting.

   ✳ Volatility3: The next-generation version of the Volatility Framework, offering enhanced memory analysis capabilities and support for a wider range of operating systems.

7. Document Analysis Tools:

   ✳ OfficeMalScanner: A tool for analyzing Microsoft Office documents (Word, Excel, PowerPoint) to detect potential malicious macros or embedded exploits.

   ✳ olevba: A Python library for analyzing Microsoft Office documents, providing the ability to extract macros, VBA code, and other embedded elements.

8. Malware Information Sharing Platforms:

   ✻ MISP: An open-source platform for sharing and collaborating on threat intelligence, facilitating the exchange of malware samples, IOCs, and analysis reports.

   ✻ VirusShare: A private malware sample repository that provides researchers with access to a vast collection of malware samples.

These tools, along with the ones mentioned in previous appendices, form a comprehensive toolbox for malware analysts. It is essential for analysts to select the appropriate tools based on their specific requirements, the nature of the malware being analyzed, and their level of expertise. Regularly exploring new tools, keeping up with updates, and staying informed about emerging technologies and analysis techniques are crucial for maintaining a strong malware analysis skill set.

APPENDIX A.4: MALWARE ANALYSIS TOOLS

Continuing from Appendices A, A.2, and A.3, here are additional commonly used tools in the field of malware analysis:

1. Dynamic Analysis Tools:

   ✻ Procmon: A Windows-based tool that monitors and captures system events, including file system activity, registry changes, and process activity.

   ✻ API Monitor: A tool for intercepting and analyzing API calls made by applications, providing insights into their behavior and potential malicious activity.

   ✻ CaptureBAT: A lightweight tool that captures and analyzes system events and behavior, helping to identify malware-related activities.

2. Threat Intelligence Platforms:

   ✻ MISP: An open-source platform for sharing, storing, and collaborating on threat intelligence, allowing analysts to exchange information about malware samples, IOCs, and analysis reports.

❋ ThreatConnect: A threat intelligence platform that aggregates and analyzes data from various sources to provide insights into malware campaigns, indicators of compromise (IOCs), and associated threat actors.

3. Code Analysis Tools:

❋ Binary Ninja: A highly extensible binary analysis platform that supports both static and dynamic analysis, enabling analysts to dissect and understand malware samples at a deep level.

❋ radare2: An open-source framework for reverse engineering and analyzing binary files, providing a wide range of features for static and dynamic analysis.

4. Sandbox Platforms:

❋ Any.Run: An interactive online malware analysis platform that allows for the safe execution and analysis of malware samples in a controlled environment.

❋ Hybrid Analysis: A cloud-based malware analysis platform that combines static and dynamic analysis techniques, providing detailed reports and behavioral insights.

5. Incident Response Tools:

❋ The Sleuth Kit: A collection of command-line tools for digital forensic analysis, including file system analysis, timeline creation, and evidence collection.

❋ Autopsy: A graphical front-end for The Sleuth Kit that simplifies the analysis of digital evidence, making it easier to investigate and analyze malware-related incidents.

6. Threat Hunting Tools:

❋ Elastic Stack (Elasticsearch, Logstash, Kibana): An open-source platform for collecting, analyzing, and visualizing log data, enabling proactive threat hunting and detection.

❋ osquery: An open-source tool that allows for querying and monitoring operating system-level events and data, aiding in the detection and analysis of malware activity.

7. Traffic Analysis Tools:

    ✻   Moloch: An open-source, large-scale, full-packet capture and indexing system for network traffic analysis, enabling the inspection of network communications related to malware activity.

    ✻   Suricata: An open-source network intrusion detection and prevention system that provides real-time analysis of network traffic, aiding in the identification of potential malware-related activities.

These tools, in combination with those mentioned in previous appendices, form a comprehensive toolkit for malware analysis. Analysts should choose the appropriate tools based on their specific needs, the type of malware being analyzed, and their level of expertise. Regularly exploring new tools, keeping up with updates, and staying informed about emerging technologies and analysis techniques are essential for effective and efficient malware analysis.

APPENDIX B: GLOSSARY OF TERMS

This glossary provides definitions for key terms and concepts used in the field of malware analysis:

1. Malware: Malicious software designed to infiltrate, damage, or gain unauthorized access to computer systems or networks.

2. Static Analysis: The examination of malware without execution, focusing on file structure, code analysis, and metadata examination.

3. Dynamic Analysis: The analysis of malware in an executing environment, observing its behavior, interactions, and effects on the system.

4. Reverse Engineering: The process of deconstructing and analyzing software to understand its design, behavior, and functionality.

5. Disassembler: A tool that translates executable code into human-readable assembly language, aiding in the analysis of program logic.

6. Debugger: A tool used to analyze and debug programs, allowing for step-by-step execution and monitoring of code.

7. Sandbox: An isolated environment that allows for the execution of potentially malicious code in a controlled manner, protecting the underlying system.

8. IOC (Indicator of Compromise): Artifacts or patterns that indicate the presence of a security incident or compromise, such as IP addresses, file hashes, or behavior patterns.

9. Packer: A tool or technique used to compress, encrypt, or obfuscate malware code, making it harder to analyze or detect.

10. Rootkit: A type of malware designed to gain unauthorized access and control over a computer system, often hiding its presence and evading detection.

11. Exploit: A piece of code or technique that takes advantage of a vulnerability or flaw in software to execute malicious actions.

12. Botnet: A network of compromised computers controlled by a central command-and-control (C&C) server, typically used for malicious activities such as distributed denial-of-service (DDoS) attacks.

13. Command-and-Control (C&C) Server: A remote server used by attackers to send commands and receive information from compromised systems.

14. Signature-based Detection: Malware detection based on predefined patterns or signatures derived from known malware samples.

15. Behavior-based Detection: Malware detection based on analyzing the behavior and actions of a program to identify suspicious or malicious activities.

16. Threat Intelligence: Information about emerging threats, attack techniques, and malicious actors used to enhance situational awareness and aid in the prevention and detection of cyber threats.

17. Indicators of Attack (IOA): Patterns or activities associated with known attack techniques, helping to identify ongoing or attempted cyber attacks.

18. Incident Response: The process of responding to and managing a security incident, including the containment, eradication, and recovery steps.

19. Threat Hunting: Proactive searching for indicators of compromise or suspicious activities within a network or system to identify and mitigate potential threats.

20. Zero-day: A previously unknown software vulnerability or exploit that has not yet been patched or addressed by the software vendor.

21. Vulnerability: A weakness or flaw in software or a system that could be exploited to compromise its security or integrity.

22. Command Injection: An attack technique where an attacker executes arbitrary commands on a target system by injecting malicious commands into an application or system command.

23. Data Exfiltration: The unauthorized extraction or theft of data from a system or network, often by malware or malicious actors.

24. Sandbox Evasion: Techniques used by malware to detect and evade detection within sandbox environments, allowing it to remain undetected or dormant.

25. Phishing: A social engineering technique where attackers impersonate legitimate entities to trick individuals into revealing sensitive information or performing malicious actions.

This glossary provides a starting point for understanding key terms in malware analysis. It is important to continually expand your knowledge and keep up with evolving terminology and concepts in the rapidly changing field of cybersecurity.

BIBLIOGRAPHY

1. Anderson, B., Quist, D., Neil, J., Storlie, C., & Lane, T. (2011). Graph-based malware detection using dynamic analysis. *Journal in Computer Virology,7*, 247-258.

2. Bayer, U., Comparetti, P. M., Hlauschek, C., Kruegel, C., & Kirda, E. (n.d.). *Scalable, Behavior-Based Malware Clustering*. Manuscript in preparation, Secure Systems Lab, Technical University Vienna.

3. Cisco Security Threat and Vulnerability Intelligence. (2014, November 10). Retrieved February 19, 2020, from https://tools.cisco.com/security/center/ resources/virus_differences

4. Cybereason. (2017). 2020 NSS Advanced Endpoint Protection & Comparative Report. Retrieved March 10, 2020, from https://www.cybereason.com/2020-nss-aep-report

5. Distler, D. (2020). Malware Analysis: An Introduction [Web log post]. Retrieved February 20, 2020, from https://www.sans.org/reading-room/whitepapers/malicious/   malware-analysis-introduction-2103

6. Martignoni L., Paleari R., Bruschi D. (2009) A Framework for Behavior-Based Malware Analysis in the Cloud. In: Prakash A., Sen Gupta I. (eds) Information Systems Security. ICISS 2009. Lecture Notes in Computer Science, vol 5905. Springer, Berlin, Heidelberg. https://doi.org/10.1007/978-3-642-10772-6_14

7. Garnaeva, M., Garnaeva, M., Wiel, J., Makrushin, D., Ivanov, A., Namestnikov, Y.,... *, N. (2015, December 15). Kaspersky Security Bulletin 2015. Overall statistics for 2015. Retrieved May 01, 2020, from https://securelist.com/kaspersky-security-bulletin-2015-overall-statistics-for-2015/73038/

8. How do I know if my computer is infected with a virus or other malware? (2018, May 13). Retrieved January 7, 2020, from https://support.eset.com/en/kb2563-how-do-i-know-if-my-computer-is-infected-with-a-virus-or-other-malware

9. Hybrid Analysis Free Automated Malware Analysis Service - powered by Falcon Sandbox. (2018, August). Retrieved February 1, 2020, from https://www.hybrid-analysis.com/

10. Introduction to x 64 Assembly. (2012, March 19). Retrieved February 19, 2020, from https://software.intel.com/content/www/us/en/develop/articles/introduction-to-x64-assembly.html

11. Jesse. (2019, October 28). 10 Symptoms of Malware Infection. Retrieved January 1, 2020, from https://softwaretested.com/anti-malware/10-symptoms-of-malware-infection/

12. K. (2020, August 26). What is Social Engineering? Retrieved May 10, 2020, from https://www.kaspersky.co.in/resource-center/definitions/what-is-social-engineering

13. K., & *. (2016, December 14). Kaspersky Security Bulletin 2016. Review of the year. Overall statistics for 2016. Retrieved May 19, 2020, from https://securelist.com/kaspersky-security-bulletin-2016-executive-summary/76858/

14. K., U., G., S., A., M. T. (2017, December 14). Kaspersky Security Bulletin. Overall statistics for 2017. Retrieved June 19, 2020, from https://securelist.com/ksb-overall-statistics-2017/83453/

15. Kaspersky. (2019, February 11). Ransomware & Cyber Blackmail. Retrieved June 19, 2020, from https://usa.kaspersky.com/resource-center/threats/ransomware

16. Kim, K. J. (2015). *Information Science and Applications*. Berlin, Heidelberg: Springer Berlin Heidelberg.

17. Kirat, D., & Vigna, G. (2015). MalGene: Automatic Extraction of Malware Analysis Evasion Signature. In *Proceedings of the 22nd ACM SIGSAC Conference on Computer and Communications Security* (pp. 769-780). New York: Association for Computing Machinery. doi:https://doi.org/10.1145/2810103.2813642

18. Kirat, D., Vigna, G., & Kruege, C. (2014, August). BareCloud: Bare-metal Analysis-based Evasive Malware Detection. In *23rd USENIX Security Symposium*. Retrieved June, 2020, from https://www.usenix.org/conference/usenixsecurity14/technical-sessions/presentation/kirat

19. Kizza, J. M. (2015). *Guide to Computer Network Security*. London: Springer London. doi:https://doi.org/10.1007/978-3-319-55606-2

20. Konrada, R., Philippb, T., Carstenb, W., & Thorstenb, H. (2011). Automatic analysis of malware behavior using machine learning. *Journal of Computer Security,19*(4), 639-668. doi:10.3233/JCS-2010-0410

21. Kupreev, O., Kupreev, O., Badovskaya, E., Gutnikov, A., & *, N. (2019). DDoS attacks in Q1 2019. Retrieved January 1, 2020, from https://securelist.com/ddos-report-q1-2019/90792/

22. Magic Quadrant Research Methodology. (2018, July). Retrieved March 11, 2020, from https://www.gartner.com/en/research/methodologies/magic-quadrants-research

23. Malenkovich, S., Grustniy, L., Aver, H., & Ferapontov, A. (2013, March 28). What is a rootkit and how to remove it. Retrieved June 11, 2020, from https://www.kaspersky.com/blog/rootkit/1508/

24. Malware 101: What is malware? (2018, June 1). Retrieved May 19, 2020, from https://us.norton.com/internetsecurity-malware.html

25. McAfee Labs 2016 Threats Predictions. (2016). Retrieved March 11, 2020, from http://34.234.105.101/wp-content/uploads/2015/11/rp-threats-predictions-2016.pdf

26. Nataraj, L., Yegneswaran, V., Porras, P., & Zhang, J. (2011). A comparative assessment of malware classification using binary texture analysis and dynamic analysis. In *Proceedings of the 4th ACM workshop on Security and artificial intelligence* (pp. 21-30). New York: Association for Computing Machinery. doi:https://doi.org/10.1145/2046684.2046689

27. Nguyen, C. Q., & Goldman, J. E. (2010). Malware analysis reverse engineering (MARE) methodology & malware defense (M.D.) timeline. In *Publication:InfoSecCD '10: 2010 Information Security Curriculum Development Conference* (pp. 8-14). Kennesaw

Georgia: Association for Computing Machinery. doi:https://doi.org/10.1145/1940941.1940944

28. O'Kane, P., Sezer, S., McLaughlin, K., & Im, E. G. (2013). SVM Training Phase Reduction Using Dataset Feature Filtering for Malware Detection. *IEEE Transactions on Information Forensics and Security,8*(3), 500-509. doi:10.1109/TIFS.2013.2242890

29. Perekalin, A., Kuksov, I., Grustniy, L., Aver, H., & Ferapontov, A. (2017, May 13). WannaCry: Are you safe? Retrieved June 19, 2020, from https://www.kaspersky.com/blog/wannacry-ransomware/16518/

30. R. (2017, May 15). Asia Reports Limited Impact of Ransomware, but Authorities Brace for More Cyberattacks. Retrieved March 19, 2020, from https://uk.news.yahoo.com/asia-reports-limited-impact-ransomware-070315210.html

31. Sikorski, M., Honig, A., & Bejtlich, R. (2012). *Practical malware analysis: The hands-on guide to dissecting malicious software.* San Francisco: No Starch Press.

32. Sinitsyn, F. (2017, November 28). Kaspersky Security Bulletin: Story of the year 2017. Retrieved January 10, 2020, from https://securelist.com/ksb-story-of-the-year-2017/83290/

33. Skoudis, E., & Zeltser, L. (2008). *Malware fighting malicious code.* Upper Saddle River, NJ: Prentice Hall PTR.

34. Skybakmoen, T., & Robin, S. (2019, March 5). ADVANCED ENDPOINT PROTECTION COMPARATIVE REPORT. Retrieved February 10, 2020, from https://secure2.sophos.com/en-us/medialibrary/gated-assets/pdf/nss-labs-aep-comparative-report-security-value-map.pdf

35. Soare, B. (2020, March 06). 13+ Warning Signs Your Computer is Infected with Malware. Retrieved April 19, 2020, from https://heimdalsecurity.com/blog/warning-signs-operating-system-infected-malware/

36. Stallings, W. (2019). *Cryptography and network security: Principles and practice* (8th ed.). Hoboken, NJ: Pearson Education.

37. Unuchek, R. (2018, March 7). Mobile malware evolution 2017. Retrieved January 11, 2020, from https://securelist.com/mobile-malware-review-2017/84139/

38. Watson, M. R., Shirazi, N., Marnerides, A. K., Mauthe, A., & Hutchison, D. (2015). Malware Detection in Cloud Computing Infrastructures. *IEEE Transactions on Dependable and Secure Computing,13*(2), 192-205. doi:10.1109/TDSC.2015.2457918

39. Watts, S. (2020, February 13). Digital Forensics and Incident Response (DFIR): An Introduction. Retrieved March 15, 2020, from https://www.bmc.com/blogs/dfir-digital-forensics-incident-response/

40. Yerima, S. Y., Sezer, S., & McWilliams, G. (2014). Analysis of Bayesian classification-based approaches for Android malware detection. *IET Information Security,8*(1), 25-36. doi:10.1049/iet-ifs.2013.0095

41. Young, A., & Yung, M. (2007). *Malicious cryptography: Exposing cryptovirology*. Indianapolis: Wiley.

42. Yusirwan, S. S., Prayudi, Y., & Riadi, I. (2015). Implementation of Malware Analysis using Static and Dynamic Analysis Method. *International Journal of Computer Applications, 117*(6), 11-15.

43. **Skoudis, E., Zeltser, L. (2004). Malware: Fighting Malicious Code. Prentice Hall.**

44. **Casey, E. (2018). Digital Evidence and Computer Crime: Forensic Science, Computers, and the Internet. Academic Press.**

45. **Ligh, M., Adair, S., Hartstein, B., & Richard, M. (2011). Malware Analyst's Cookbook and DVD: Tools and Techniques for Fighting Malicious Code. Wiley.**

46. **Mandiant. (2020). M-Trends 2020: The Advanced Persistent Threat Landscape. Mandiant, a FireEye company.**

47. **Szor, P. (2005). The Art of Computer Virus Research and Defense. Pearson Education.**

48. **Russinovich, M. E., Solomon, D. A., & Ionescu, A. (2012). Windows Internals, Part 1: System architecture, processes, threads, memory management, and more. Microsoft Press.**

49. Eilam, E. (2005). Reversing: Secrets of Reverse Engineering. Wiley.

50. Mandiant. (2018). Reverse Engineering Malware: A Hands-On Approach. FireEye Threat Intelligence.

51. Rouse, M. (2020). Dynamic Analysis (Dynamic Testing). TechTarget.

52. Bishop, M. (2003). Computer Security: Art and Science. Addison-Wesley Professional.